Courtney Barrett

MW01170229

stay strong in your journey
†

FRONT BOOK COVER PHOTO RECAP:

IN THIS PHOTO, BOTH OF MY GIRLS USED ONE BIG BAG

TO COLLECT ALL THE LEGOS THAT WERE FOUND IN THE DEBRIS

CAUSED BY IRMA. THEY END UP WITH A LARGE COLLECTION.

YOU WILL READ ABOUT IT LATER ON IN THE STORY, ALL

THANKS TO A SPECIAL FAMILY.

(THANK YOU CAMERON WALDERA AND WALDERA FAMILY)

AUTHOR:

COURTNEY BARRETT MACIAS

PHOTOS PROVIDED BY:

MARATHON FL. KEYS COMMUNITY

DEDICATED

TO THE FLORIDA KEYS,

TO ALL THOSE WHO LOST THEIR

LIFE, LOVED ONES, AND THOSE WHO

WERE AFFECTED

BY IRMA

SPECIAL THANKS TO

MY MOM FOR GIVING ME THE IDEA TO WRITE THIS BOOK
AND FULFILL IT TO REALITY

DAYS BEFORE
IRMA

MONDAY SEPTEMBER 4, 2017

At 8:21 a.m. I'm at my girl's school while they are eating their breakfast. I check my cell phone to see a new update of Hurricane IRMA. It's now covering parts of the Bahamas and Cuba while sitting at a category 3. By later today we will know if it's coming right for us. As Ariel and Leona finish their breakfast, I think of how they will handle the aftermath of the storm. My girls are aware of the hurricane; they know that we will be leaving in the next few days if it comes. Knowing this storm will most likely hit here, makes me nervous for all of our friends, families, and our whole community. Ariel and Leona finish their breakfast and we exchange hugs and kisses. Ariel (my older daughter) tells me, "Mommy I hope the storm isn't coming because I want to be able to have my school and classroom. I don't want the storm to take it away." Ariel gives me an extra hug and heads off to her class line up.

By 10:30 a.m. I'm at work with my husband at Lazy Days South. Lazy Days is an ocean front restaurant located on 11th street, in Marathon, on the Atlantic side. It's well known for their seafood and amazing food preparations. We both have worked here for several years as servers. Today is really slow, because of the storm heading this way. We have had the Weather Channel on all day. The Weather Channel says the new update will be at 5:00 p.m. We all wait. 4:30 p.m. comes around and my shift is over. I head towards my mom's house to pick up my girls. Upon my arrival I notice it's about 5:00 p.m. I check my cell and there was the update. My heart drops and my head spins. The cone is centered right over Marathon and marked as a category 4. I run into my mom's home. I throw her door open in a panic just to see that, they too, are glued to the update. All of the Keys are watching the news. We know it's definitely time to think of our evacuation plans. My kids and I leave my mom's. As I arrive home at 5:25 p.m. I check my cell. A weather alert came on my phone stating "STATE OF EMERGENCY NOW DECLARED FOR FLORIDA." My panic mode is rising. We have a couple of days to decide where to go, how to close up our home, what to pack, do we have enough gas? Do we pack food? Is our car reliable

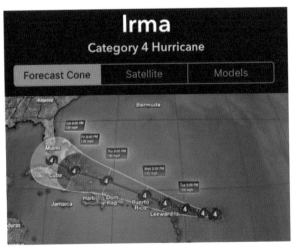

to make a drive out of Florida? Millions of more questions fill my head, on what do we do? I call my friend Angela to speak with her on the "State of Emergency." She told me that they are starting to get their ideas going of how to close up their home. She's thinking of maybe staying. We said we will keep each other updated as we make our choices and choose where to go next. My kids and I walk into our house to start our daily routine. I call my husband Jose for some advice on what we should do next. He advises the girls and I to go to Home Depot and look for gas cans ASAP. The girls and I quickly head over there. We start running through aisles looking for cans. There weren't any. I asked an employee if they had any more hidden in the back and she said, "What you see is what we have, sorry." I call my husband back and tell him there is none here. He tells me that nowhere else will have them, so we better go get gas into the car and fill up now. I go fill up the tank and as I'm pumping gas, he calls me again. He reminds me that we should get re-entry stickers to make it easier to get back into Marathon. I look at the time and see that it's too late to go now. We agree that tomorrow we will go in the a.m. and get stickers so we have no issues coming back through the Keys. As I finish pumping gas, I notice that all of us at the pumps, were all on cell phones. Everyone was talking about the hurricane and that there may be a gas shortage soon here in the Keys. I head home with the girls.

At 9:30 p.m. Jose calls me to come pick him up from work. All the employees left early due to the storm coming. When we got home we discussed the big questions that everyone is talking about. Do we stay with friends, family, or a hotel? How far do we go and what direction? How do we secure all our belongings? Do we try to leave as a group with other family we have here in the Keys? Whose side of the family do we evacuate with? How much money will we spend? How long should we plan to be gone for? Do we take both vehicles? We then remember that our other vehicle, 2003 Ford Explorer, is at our friend's home in Long Key. Twenty minutes is far when you don't have the means of gas to go get it and bring it back to your home. Jose was working on a job two days ago with his friend, Chris, who had dropped him off at home saving him to make a drive. We notify Chris on the gas situation and he said its fine for us to leave it there. The down fall is that his home is waterfront and our explorer could take a loss from the upcoming damages. We decide to take our chances; we go to bed ready to take on new challenges for tomorrow.

VALLEJO FAMILY

Angela woke up and saw the weather report of Irma covering parts of the Bahamas and Cuba. She thought it would go off to the east, therefore she wasn't even worried for the storm to hit.

Angela has a son named Isaak who is friends with my daughter Ariel. Our kids play soccer together. She got him up and ready for school. She wasn't thinking the storm would be a big deal and wasn't in fear for school closing yet. As usual, she took him to school.

Angela had gone to Home Depot a few days ago for gas containers and flash lights. They were wanting to stay because they thought it wouldn't really come here. " We may get a swipe an it'll stay east", she thought. Angela bought the last two red flashlights available. The place was packed with people. She grabbed what she thought they would need since the family was planning to stay behind.

At home her animals were acting strange. The Dog didn't want to go outside. The cat was showing fear in her daily routine. The animals could sense something wasn't right. This made her question what may be coming.

After getting Isaak from school at 3:30 p.m. Angela and Isaak went to Publix to load up on water and can goods to be able to stay home during the storm.

Near 5:00 p.m. – "Declared State of Emergency" came across her TV. She immediately called me to let me know of this new notice. She was still unsure that it would really come. Angela and her husband Started to get shutters out and nail them up just in case. They loaded up their house with items to be prepared for no electricity here in the Keys. She started to get all important documents and family memories together to have packed, that they didn't want ruined. Later on they looked at the TV and saw it was coming as a category 5. Angela prayed that it would go away. She kept saying that we have been so lucky; but deep inside, she kind of knew that it was too good to be true that this monster would go away.

BEN AND KRISTEN

DAYS EARLIER Ben and Kristen saw the weather, days in advance and noticed that Irma is one storm to be looking out for. This one will develop to be big. Ben knew this one was going to be a problem and Kristen was reassuring him that he was wrong. She was sure it would go away.

Ben and Kristen work at the Sea Dell Motel in Marathon. It's a very cute motel located on the gulf side. Ben does a lot of maintaining of the property. Kristen is the manager for the front desk. Kristen had mentioned, to the motel owner, that Irma may strike the Keys. The motel owner, Harry, had told Kristen it'll be fine and it'll be just like last year when hurricane Matthew came through. It'll just fizzle out to nothing before coming here. So she believed him.

MONDAY Irma became a monster out in the middle of nowhere. The European model said it was coming to the Keys when it was still 6 days out. "The European model has always been accurate," quotes Ben. Today Ben started preparing. Rick Ramsey (our sheriff) said, "If you are staying, make sure you are part of the solution and not part of the problem." Kristen didn't believe anything she was hearing about Irma.

Ben was on a job painting a home for a client and then later quits painting after a news update. He packs up and heads home. It is 6 days before the storm comes ashore, Ben was taking buckets (5-gallon pails each) from his own home and started to clean them all. He filled up 100 gallons of water, and 35 gallons of potable water. Kristen thought he was a loser for doing all this and stopping his job. He had told her if we decide to stay, we need to plan for the worse and hope for the best. He got crappy buckets for toilet water so they can flush. He stored 65 gallons of water, for showering and other things. He was getting his wife and himself prepared, as he sees it is coming.

The Sea Dell Motel has made it through every hurricane since the 1950's. Harry, the owner, didn't believe Irma would actually come. Ben, thought differently and starts bagging lots of ice from the motel ice dispenser. Ben and Kristen both knew they wouldn't stay at their home. They thought of Hurricane Wilma which brought in a lot of storm surge. Their home flooded during Hurricane Wilma. So he went out and bought 2X4's and 4X8 sheets of plywood and cinder blocks to bring home. Together the two of them put all their worldly possessions 5-feet above the ground. They built platforms. It was like scaffolding. TVs, dressers, beds, furniture, dishes, everything was high up. The most important things were even higher up. Their items were touching their 9-foot ceiling. Nothing was below 5-feet, that way they had a chance of beating the storm surge heights. If Irma's waters go higher than that, then they know it'll all come crashing down and so be it. He duck taped all opening areas in door crevices.

Kristen is over here thinking, "You are doing this for nothing. Irma will go up to Cuba and go out. It won't happen to me. "

Ben was working on a job for the McFalls. These people are so gracious. They asked them if they were staying behind. Ben said yes we are staying. They said, "Well if you would feel more secure at the

ocean house, you're more than welcome to stay there." They're clients of Bens. Their home sits right on the gulf side, and literally has the water front view. This home used to be owned by the Sea Dell Motel but was just sold months ago to the McFall's. Ben maintains the home for them, since he knows the home so well from when it was owned by the motel. The home sits approximately 15-feet above sea level on stilts. This home was just inspected for insurance purposes for hurricanes and it's good to go. He thanked them for the offer and said he will let them know what they decide.

Ben has been at the motel and some other spots for 5 days now preparing for the storm. Kristen has just been shaking her head at Ben and calling him a loser for over preparing.

At the motel Harry keeps telling her," It's just a big hype to kill tourism." He wasn't making it a big deal at all. He wasn't pushing anyone to close up the motel or start to prepare the outside of the structure for a hurricane that won't come.

Later today, all the employees left the motel. There was no one to clean rooms. Kristen was alone from Monday evening on. Now she's starting to think, "Okay, this is real because everyone has up and left me. Ryan, my number one guy, waved at me in the parking lot and didn't even say bye. He just got into his car, left and that was it from him. Now my heart is pounding as this is really happening. Then there were the tourism evacuations and the motel is emptied out. Then what happens? We start to get the local homeless coming by. It was a mess."

TUESDAY SEPTEMBER 5, 2017

On the way to school this morning Leona was crying. She doesn't want to be separated from all her friends, or have to leave her classroom and teacher. She was sad for everyone having to leave soon and grab what they can take with them. It's sad to see our kids get emotional over this. As we wait in the lunch line, the girls are mingling with their close friends. They're all talking about the storm. Kids are asking each other where they're going and when they're leaving. The kids were all hugging each other while saying their goodbyes, because they don't know when they'll all be together again. So sad to witness this. It makes you want to cry for them. I did hope they're going to cancel school for tomorrow. The storm is approaching fast and it doesn't make since for kids to still go. We will probably be leaving Wednesday. I say bye to the girls as they eat their breakfast. I head for home. It was time for Jose and I to start another chaotic day.

Near 10:00 a.m. Jose and I arrive at the sheriff's office for our blue re –entry stickers. You get two stickers per person. We got ours and saved an extra for our other family members to get back into the Keys. We place a sticker on our car windshield. This car will have to be the one that gets us out and back into the Keys.

By noon I receive a text message from Leona's teacher letting me know that schools have been canceled in the Keys tomorrow until further notice. That's a relief. We all need to get out of the Keys. I notify Angela about the school message. She had just heard it announced on the local TV news.

Jose and I decide to drive over to Lazy Days and let them know that school is closing which means we are about to hear an evacuation notice at any time. As we walk in the door we see all the employees and management hanging around at the hostess stand. We tell them that we have decided to leave in the morning for northern Florida and we won't be at work tomorrow as scheduled. Management is still deciding when to close. I tell them that many places are closing already. We watched them boarding up as we drove by. Our manager agreed with us that they should close soon because they'll have no employees here to work for the restaurant. We offered to help them close but they don't know when that would be. We told them if they can't close today then we won't be here to help them. Our family and kids come first so we are leaving.

I looked around and noticed that my sister, Megan, wasn't here with the employees. The hostess tells me Megan left early as she plans to leave tonight. I hadn't been told by her or any of my family that they plan on leaving in the next few hours. My sister and her husband both work with us at Lazy Days. I call my sister Megan and she tells me that Monroe County just put out a tourist evacuation shortly before she left. She said a customer came in to eat and he had told her about the evacuation notice and he would like his food to go. That's when Megan knew it was time to leave. We finish our conversation and hang up. My sister and her husband might come by our place later tonight to drop off their personal items. We are in a 3-story building made of concrete and up to hurricane codes. My sister lives on the Gulf side by the water and she's ground level. Their home structure is iffy. It has made it through past storms, but IRMA will be a true test.

Our manager on duty was flipping out over the situation. She didn't know what to do. The owner had told her to try and stay open till Friday. No one will even be in the Keys by then. Our manager said, "Well if there's no employees then we can't stay open. We can't make them stay."

Many employees all over the Keys had left their jobs early. Several left before their owners or managers wanted them to. The concern of being fired ran through the minds of many I know, myself included. We had to do what was safe for our families and that was to leave. Many of the conversations on Marathons social network page was about employees asking if it's against the law to fire workers who leave for hurricanes when we aren't told by our jobs that we can. I don't know the answer to this. My husband and I did have our jobs when we came back, even though we did bail early. I can't speak for others.

Our manager hopes to close tomorrow. She knows we all need time to close up before the storm. Jose and I wished them all the best and told them we will see them sometime after the storm. Lazy Days ended up closing on Wednesday September 6th. All of the kitchen crew helped to close up the restaurant.

Jose and I drive home quickly to get money from our apartment so we can go to the bank. We know this is no joke and we don't know how much time we have for places to be open. We have been saving all of our one and five dollar bills into a bucket at home. This is what we normally use for vacation money every year but now it'll be our evacuation money instead. We go to the bank to get larger bills. There are long lines of people. There was a man there talking to a teller and he was talking about how he just bought a home in Little Torch Key. He has put in over $100,000 into landscaping. He knows he will be taking a huge loss and insurance won't be able to help back. Everyone has a story to tell of what they are in fear of. Due to IRMA coming our way, people are sharing their situations left and right. No matter where you are, it was all we could talk about.

We get the girls from school near 3:00 p.m. and head home. Ariel changes once more for her last karate class till after the storm. She has class as usual. After class they all had hugs exchanged and said their good byes till next time. Ariel tells me how much she will miss her class and everyone in it. She hopes and prays for all her "Ookie" friends (name for your buddies in karate class). She hopes her karate class will be okay. She would be sad if classes never resumed.

At home I check my app at 5:15 p.m. and see that IRMA is coming to the Keys head on as a category 5. My heart drops more as this becomes more surreal that we really need to leave and hope for the best for Marathon. We all start packing our suitcases. Jose fed our snake. She will be good for a few weeks because sadly we can't take her. I fed our fish. We gather up all our dog supplies to take Rascal, our Boston Terrier, with us. We pack all weather clothes. We don't know where we may end up. Jose plans for Gainesville and then we will decide after that.

My sister and her husband, Todd, appear near 6:00 p.m. to drop off their most prized possessions. My sister offers for me to come by our mom's house before they all leave in two hours. While Jose finishes packing, I rush off to my mom's home with a birthday present in hand. I arrive with Ariel and Leona and we run inside. My mom and family asks for us to come along with them. They're going to Tallahassee Florida. They'll decide where to go after that. I told them we aren't leaving till mid-day tomorrow because we are staying back to help our friend, Chris. He has an outdoor place and he needs our help putting everything away. When we are done there, then we will leave. My mom called me crazy.

While there, we say hi to my niece Riley and nephew Beckham. Beckham is turning 1 on Sunday, the day Irma will hit. My sister had purchased cute themed items of the Hungry Caterpillar. She will be taking them with her and celebrating the birthday during this evacuation to wherever we end up. Beckham opens his gift. It was a "Jack in the Box "from Hungry Caterpillar. Beckham had no expression when he opened it. I've seen many online videos of babies laughing and crying. He didn't do either one. I wasn't expecting his blank stare. We all say bye to each other. The girls and I head home while the guys start packing up all the vehicles they're taking. I told the family that we will meet up with them at our final destination when its known.

I do a last minute gas fill up on the car in Marathon. I now have enough to get to Ft. Lauderdale. Our gas plan is to start looking at the halfway point. We know gas stations will have long lines, be scarce, or empty. One gas station by my apartment already had one pump bagged. That's never a good sign. It's becoming more real.

Near 8:00 p.m. we call Jose's family. We will stop by their home on the way out in Key Largo. We may be able to travel with them.

Jose and I make our last minute checklist for tomorrow. We know how to protect our windows and save the plants. Tomorrow we will unplug things, set the AC to a warmer temp, and we should be good to go. (We didn't think to empty the fridge and freezer; this was our first evacuation). Happy with our progress of today, we go to bed really tired knowing it will be a long day tomorrow.

(All packed and ready for tomorrow)

VALLEJO FAMILY

This morning Angela took Isaak to school, since there's no canceling of school yet. Near noon she got a message about School cancelation for all of Monroe county. "Okay this is getting real something bad is going to come now" she said to herself. Fear in everyone's eyes started to show all over the area. Angela started asking all other moms what their plans are. Are others staying or choosing to go? When are they are leaving? Where are they going? She started to ask herself, "Do we go to Miami to stay with family? This storm now seems too close. We need to go more north to Orlando."

Angela called her sister for advice and they together agreed to look for housing in Orlando. Her sister later found a place for them all, including their pets. It took 8 hours to find and book a room. Thanks to West Gate Hotel for having space for the whole family. Angela, her husband, their son and more family will all be leaving for Orlando in the next day or so.

They spent their time packing most of the day to leave in their van. All their important papers, pictures, items not to be left behind, were all packed as well.

EVACUATE

OR

STAY ?

WEDNESDAY SEPTEMBER 6, 2017

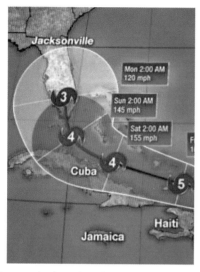

I wake at 2:25 a.m. to see IRMA will be heading to the east coast of Florida. That would be great if that happens, then it won't hit us. I wasn't able to stay asleep knowing this storm is approaching so quick. I close my eyes and fall back to sleep. I wake again at 7:03 a.m. IRMA is now heading straight up into the middle of Florida. No more going off to the east. She's going to cut Florida right in half. The eye may go right over Key Largo and miss a bit of Marathon. This is going to be bad. I get Jose and the kids up. We start packing up the car and protect our windows in the apartment on the inside. I Don't know how much good this will do if the storm breaks the window. It makes us feel better knowing we can protect our things a little. No storm shutters are given for our apartment on the outside. We take a big piece of sturdy plexi glass that we happen to have, and we put it across the girls' bedroom window. We push their bunkbed against it to help to hold it into place. We took our mattress and put it against our living room sliding glass window. We moved a large heavy exercising machine against the mattress to hold it into place as well. We brought in all our outdoor plants in hopes that they may survive the weeks we won't be here. We finish our last minute ideas to protect some other windows. We unplug all appliances except the fridge and stove. Jose left the AC on at 86 to keep some type of air circulation in the home until it does go out. It didn't come to mind to empty our fridge. Checking around the home for anything we may have left out, we say good bye to the fish, Layla the snake, and then we shut our door. Time to head for the car.

In the car we double check all our items once more. The girls showed us that we were stocked on our lunch boxes, snacks, and drinks. We drive over to Walgreens for some ice. Next we head over to a friend's outdoor restaurant by 9:30 a.m. He was so close to opening his new place. Now we need to put all the furniture away and all other items that could be damaged from the storm. I stay for almost an hour and I see that this will take a few more hours. The girls and I head over to my mom's house. My whole family had left yesterday but I have a key to get into their home. Jose stays to help his friend. The girls play in the play room at my mom's while I stay glued to the Weather Channel the whole time we were there. My mom calls me to ask where I am at 1:00 p.m. I tell her I am at her house and she freaks, they're in Tallahassee FL. They are planning to stay there tonight again; they were there last night as well. I told her I don't know when we are leaving but I'll let her know when we do. She asked where we planned to go when we leave and again I said I don't know. We are still planning to stop in Key Largo by his brothers to see what their plans are. I told my mom I'll keep them updated. By 2:30 p.m. I get a call and Jose is done. The girls and I leave moms to get Jose so we can head towards Key Largo. Our friend thanks us as we go. He plans to leave tomorrow because he still needed to pack away his home up for what's coming.

We arrive to Key Largo by almost 4:00 p.m. Many roads are being set up with cones as a one-way exit. Some 4 -way stop lights were already blinking for all of us to keep going north. There wasn't an easy way to go south. We arrive to Jose's brothers house and we go in to speak with them. His brother, wife, and two kids were all finishing up their packing. They tell us that they have another family of four joining them on the evacuation. None of them have any clue of where to go. Jessie is the sister –in- law of my husband Jose. She and her friend had been making calls for hours. They haven't had any luck finding any places open for eight people. If we join them, we are adding a dog and four more people. Now we need a place for 12 and a dog. It'll be nearly impossible to find a place for all of us last minute. I brought my laptop out and started to search for places. No luck for the state of Florida, Georgia, Carolinas, Louisiana, Alabama or Tennessee; and no luck anywhere! It's hard to find a spot for so many of us at such short notice and a dog. The few we did find were too pricy or didn't allow pets. We searched hotels, resorts, rental homes, and many other types of accommodations. We are all on a budget and didn't want to spend so much on an evacuation.

Minutes later Jessie got a call from a family member who has a home in Hialeah, not far from Key Largo. They have a seasonal home that is vacant at this time. So we all talk about it. We decide that it's best for them to go with their friends because it'll sleep all eight of them. Pets aren't allowed into the condo. We tell Jose's family that its best we split up and let them go. We say our goodbyes and tell each other we will meet up again after the storm passes. We left their home a little after 4:30 p.m. to head to northern Florida. We didn't know a destination yet but we just decided to drive until we find out where we should stop.

Soon as we leave the Keys, we drive onto the long stretch. It's 18-miles of nothing until you reach Florida City. This is always such a drag. It's nothing but water and swamp marshes for 20-minutes or so. I call my family to see what their plans are, hoping it'll help tell us where we should be going. My mom answers and says they're staying again tonight in Tallahassee as planned. They can only stay one more night. They have to leave tomorrow because their hotel is booked with people staying there for the storm. We all have to find a new destination. I start mentioning Tennessee to make it a vacation, or save money and find family to stay with. I tell my mom I'll call her back. I start calling people I know in Virginia and Alabama. We have family and friends in both states. My sister calls, telling me her plans of going to Virginia to see our dad and friends. I told her we had thought about that, but now the storm may go a little that way. The Carolinas and parts of Georgia are now under evacuation too. It's too far for us to go that way. I told Megan that Jose and I may go to Alabama to see our life long family friends. I call our friends in Alabama and they opened their home for us to stay there. After so many calls back and forth for 20-minutes on that long stretch, we finally decided that we would go to Alabama. As soon as we reach the Turnpike in Florida City we map our cell phones to Alabama. I call my mom and she too had been on the phone with our friends in Alabama planning the same thing. My family found a hotel for all of them to stay at. Myself, Jose, and the girls will be staying at our friend's home. My sister decided she may still go to Virginia anyway because her friends and our dad really want them there. I guess we will see what they choose when tomorrow comes around. We were going to spend the night in Gainesville but all hotels are full. We are taking on the 11 hour trip all the way through. It will be longer than 11 hours with the entire state of Florida evacuating. As we entered the Turnpike we saw many gas stations with lines along the road. It's starting already an we are at the bottom of the state. This will be interesting, I thought.

picture above: Florida City as you enter onto the Florida Turnpike from the Keys.

At 8:00 p.m. we pass by Boynton Beach. There was traffic galore for hours ahead of us. The app on my cell was able to show me how far the traffic was ahead and many details about it. We are in for the 10 MPH drive for the next hour or so. 1 hour and 30-minutes later we are still moving 10-20 MPH. This highway is 4 lanes of traffic. As we approach the traffic ending, our lanes became three lanes of moving traffic and the fourth lane is stopped. A mile and a half later, we see why there was one lane of stopped traffic that created 4 lanes of traffic for hours. All these people were waiting for the Pompano Beach Plaza stop. I hope this plaza has enough gas for all of these miles of cars. We have enough to get to Ft. Lauderdale. We are looking for gas as we approach half a tank. The Pompano Beach Plaza was the same one my family went to last night on their way up. They had sent me a picture of them all in traffic for over 40-minutes to get their gas. My step dad is pulling his new boat behind their truck which, will cause them to have more gas stops. The boat is brand new. They didn't want to take that loss.

Later on we come upon more traffic down the road. This time I'm doing the driving. We swapped drivers on the road a while back. My husband and kids are asleep. Time is nearing 11:00 p.m. or so. I have driven for 3 hours and my distance only covered us to 1 hour and 30-minutes closer to our destination. That's how slow traffic in 4 lanes is progressing. I decided to change the route and take the detour given on my cell to avoid all this traffic. I woke Jose and he agreed for us to chance it. As we took an exit, I look behind us and see that many cars had the same idea as us. According to our GPS, it'll be over an hour before we can have an option to join back into the highway. As we travel along these dark back roads we only see the moons light guiding us with our headlights. We are following cars that are headed north and cars are following behind us. It's just a line of flowing traffic going north and an empty road going south. It was one lane each way. Some areas in the back roads were smooth and other spots were rough. We saw many bumper to bumper accidents. Those cars had their hazard lights on and people were checking their bumpers for damage. Their cars were loaded to the top with luggage as we are all out driving for the same reasons. People were following way to close throughout this whole trip. We were on this back road for almost two hours.

We are looking for gas as we're getting lower. There were no gas stations open at all. If we were on the main highway, gas wouldn't be an issue. Waiting for it would be time consuming. We passed by many small towns. The ones that did happen to be open, in the middle of nowhere, they were lit up and had bags on the pumps. Some gas stations had cops to make sure no one entered. There was caution tape surrounding one whole gas station because they were out completely. Other gas stations, when we got to the larger towns, had lines over a mile long stretching down one road. There were cops directing traffic and the cars to each pump. It was so chaotic. We skipped all of these and kept on driving for another choice. I pull over for Jose to drive and take on the madness.

We came upon one station. We were lucky to have no line. We were wondering why no one else was here. All these open pumps were great. We see a diesel pick- up truck pumping gas. Jose pulls up behind him. The man asked if we were planning on putting diesel gas into our car. We told him no. He says to us that its diesel only and that we need to keep driving down the road some more. He mentioned he saw some open with short lines. We leave to look for these stations. Well if we had a diesel truck we would've been in good hands with gas. Finally, we found one. He was right, but again the line was so long we couldn't see the end of it. We keep driving.

30-minutes pass by and still no gas. It's getting lower. We see a gas station and pull in. We see all the cars doing the same but they all circled the place and then left in search for more gas. All the pumps were bagged here too. Jose parks the car. It's pouring rain now. I was going to walk the dog while Jose makes the girls sandwiches, but there was too much rain. It's now Midnight.

VALLEJO FAMILY

All day today Angela and her husband were Lifting furniture onto cinder blocks. Their goal is to leave Thursday morning. They remembered to empty their fridge and freezer completely. Angela knew the storm was going to come hard. Her and her husband Alex rushed to try and get all items from outside to be secured indoors. They were preparing their home for the storm and doing last minute things they needed to do before evacuating. They will be leaving in the middle of the night while the roads are quiet.

BEN AND KRISTEN

They were offered to stay at the ocean house the other day. They decided to take the proposition. Back at the motel Kristen was at the front desk working. Some man came in with money wanting a room and he somehow had no idea that there was a hurricane coming and was wanting to check in. He wasn't all there in the head mentally. Kristen asked if he knew about hurricane Irma. This man didn't have a clue about any storms. His reply was, "Well I haven't seen nor checked any papers since 1990." They allow him into a room at the motel for the night.

Later Ben and Kristen start to move things into the water front home. They hunkered down. Both of them brought all the gallons of water, clothes, can goods, and coolers packed with food. Ben says to Kristen, "This is where we are staying till this whole thing ends." They filled the freezers as well. When the power does go out, they'll make their choice as to which coolers the food will be moved into from the freezers. They had milk, cheese, butter, and more stored.

The motel was still open. Kristen carried around the motel phone in case they needed to answer a call. She had seen people boarding up around her. Some were writing on the ply boards "Screw you IRMA" and others saying things similar to that. Kristen noticed that the town was deserted. Later that night a man named Dave needed a room last minute. He was planning on staying till Monday. They put him in the safest room possible. He had 2 little dogs with him. He had seemed to be ok. Ben and Kristen go back to the ocean house and get everything ready for the storm. Later that night they were all set for what's to come. They're ready for tomorrows long work day at the motel.

THURSDAY SEPTEMBER 7, 2017

At midnight I run, in the pouring rain, into the gas station. I asked the lady behind the counter where the closest gas station was. Then quickly asked her if she knew where there would be gas in them. She replies to me that one travel plaza just filled up with gas about 30-minutes ago. She told me how to get there and we were only 10-minutes away. I run back to the car and tell Jose how to get there. Jose made me a sandwich. I ate it on the way as we find this other gas station. The lady's directions were accurate as we pull up into the line of the gas station. We had about 10 cars ahead of us. It was still raining but not pouring. I get out to walk our dog while we wait our turn to get gas. 4 cops were there. 2 cops were directing cars to the pumps. 2 cops were by the door entrance. Cop cars were along the gas station with their lights flashing. We were in and out within 20-minutes.

After all of this we decided no more back roads. As we start driving, we search for the main road again. These back roads were crazy. Near 2:00 a.m. we get back onto the main highway. At 4:00 a.m. we came into Lake City FL. Traffic is barely moving when we see a rest area next to us that had reached the max capacity. Cops were waving the cars to keep moving away from the entrance lane. Passing a rest area, we saw a line of cars parked all on the top of the hill of the rest area. Families getting out to stretch, while others were running down the hill towards the bathroom. This closed rest stop caused over an hour of traffic. Passing more of the rest stop we see over a mile of stopped vehicles on the road side beyond the rest area. People were still getting out and walking that distance to go there. It was wild to see.

Nearing 5:00 a.m. we see another rest area. Vehicles were packed into the lot, the road side, and wherever people could find spots. This one was open but it was just as chaotic looking. No cops were monitoring this one that I could see. 6:00 a.m. we arrive in Tallahassee Fl. My family is all here in some hotel nearby. We didn't call them. We would like to stay overnight being as tired as we are but we will drive all the way to Montgomery. We get off the exit to look for gas. We use our cell to map gas stations close to us. We go by 8 of them and every one was out of gas. Many gas stations had caution tape around the pumps and cops guarding the space. Spotting a breakfast house, we decide to go in and eat. We haven't eaten a meal, other than packed sandwiches and snacks, since Tuesday night. If we search for more gas stations here we will be able to fill up and make it all the way to Montgomery Al.

Sitting down, we order our food and search like we never have before for gas. I searched things like "Gas stations that have gas in Tallahassee." Somehow I came across a site I have never heard before. This site saved us. It showed us exactly where to go, how long ago someone was there, and if there was gas there. I jump up from the table and tell Jose to order for me and I'll be back. I up and leave the family to race over as if everyone else was headed in the same direction for the same place as me. Once I arrived at the gas station, only premium was left but that works for us. I was able to fill the tank all the way up and go back to my family. They were done eating by the time I got back. I was gone around 15-minutes or so. I quickly ate mine there and took the rest to go. Glad this stop worked out well for us. Jose and I were both surprised to still see so many gas places empty this far north.

We start our few hours we have left to Alabama. I'm driving as they are all asleep again. I see the Alabama sign at 8:00 a.m. in a little town. I got excited and pulled the car over to take a picture. I Drove through many little towns once we entered Alabama. We are only 3 hours or less away now. Almost there finally.

11:00 a.m. we get into Montgomery Alabama. Yay hills. It was a nice change of scenery other than ocean water. Tractors, farms, cows, fields, cooler weather, wow what a different experience. So glad we packed all types of weather clothes. I call my family at 11:30 a.m. and they're still at their hotel. They will be here later on today. They all wanted to take their time and sleep in. Jose and I are so tired we are on adrenaline. Minutes later, almost at noon, we pull into our friend's drive way. Abigail, her brother Aaron, their parents Harry, and Gwen have been long time family friends of my family for over 30 years. We go into their back yard to see Harry cleaning out their pool. He asked us how our journey was getting here. We gave him the long story. Harry suggests us to get settled in and leave our dog here. He recommended some places for us to get lunch. We got to see Aaron minutes later and said hi. He's the same age as my sister. Abigail and I are the same age too. Gwen and Abigail are working at their jobs. We drove by Abigail's home to see if her husband David was there but he was working. Time to venture out and find some food, which we did. After lunch we found a home outdoor department store. Walking in we found the jackpot of gas containers. They were on the highest shelf possible. We called someone over with a forklift to get them down for us. A few other people behind us in the aisle asked for a few as well. We took the three largest ones we saw. I was so happy to have these. They will be needed when we go back into the Keys.

Jose stops at a gas station to fill all the containers. We stop by a few stores to grab other items that we forgot to pack. Hours later all my family shows up at Abigail's moms home. Gwen and Harry are so kind to take Jose, myself, and the girls in. We will be sleeping in the living room. My family all came in to say hi. They are all staying in a hotel for their time here. Many hotels are booked from evacuees. We all go outside to take group pictures together. Afterwards Jose and I take our girls, and niece Riley, to a local playground. Time to run off all the energy that has been kept inside. At the park I spoke with another mom asking if she knew other playgrounds nearby. Come to find out she wasn't from here either. She was here with her son and husband from Homestead. How wild is that. They're just here for the night because they couldn't find a hotel open for more than just tonight. They plan to leave tomorrow for Texas to be with family and wait out the storm.

Later we go back to Gwen's where we all play games. My mom and Gwen go grocery shopping, and later make dinner. It was a nice day but also very tiring. I was excited when it was bed time because I was struggling to stay awake all day.

women pictured below: from left to right

Abigail, myself (Courtney), My sister(Megan), my mom(Dodie), Gwen, my girls (Leona and Ariel). My niece (Riley) didn't want to get in the picture. Baby Beckham also not pictured here.

Guys pictured below: left to right

Jose (my husband), Aaron, Todd (my brother in law), David (my step dad), and Richard (my step brother), Harry (Gwen's husband) not pictured.

TOGETHER AGAIN WITH FAMILY AND LIFELONG FRIENDS. TIME TO WAIT FOR

IRMA TO PASS. WE PLAYED MANY GAMES.

BEN AND KRISTEN

Kristen had a hair appointment this morning. She got a call from her hair dresser Amy that she had also left and deserted her. So now Kristen had to deal with REAL gray hair for another month.

Ben and Kristen start closing up the motel by 11:00 a.m. and securing the motels pool area. They asked Harry If they should start to cover all windows and sliding glass doors. Harry still assumed it wasn't coming and it'll all be fine. Nothing got boarded up, no doors, windows, or sliding glass fixtures. Harry said, "Just put all the furniture in one motel room." She felt so deserted there. The wind wasn't even blowing. It was dead calm. No one was around. "It was such an eerie feeling" said Kristen. Thursday night was the last time anything was open. You're in trouble if you missed anything you needed. Kristen's anxiety at this point was raising sky high.

Minutes later they got homeless people that came back to harass them at the motel. Ben and Kristen told them to get to the busses so they could leave. Kristen had called the homeless peoples families so their families could be re-assured that these people needed to be evacuated. Ben and Kristen told them they had to leave and they had no choice. Kristen made sure the homeless understood why they could not stay. The homeless people, got to the busses and headed out.

Dave had paid till Sunday so he could stay. Ben and Kristen had told him if he needed anything that he could call them and stay with them at the beach house. He thanked them for the heads up and stays at the motel. Ben and Kristen go back to the ocean house for the night.

Tonight, the old man from yesterday had booked tonight to stay again.

THE VALLEJOS EVACUATE

FURNITURE ABOVE TO HOPEFULLY AVOID WATER

ALL PACKED AND READY TO EVACUATE

TIME TO LEAVE TO ORLANDO

THE HOME IS SECURE FOR IRMA

DURING THE STORM

WATER COMES
UP TO THE
LIVING ROOM
WINDOW

FRIDAY SEPTEMBER 8ᵀᴴ, 2017

11:00 a.m. I see IRMA is moving more west. The eye is headed more for Marathon and Big Pine Key area.

By noon the trail is headed for Montgomery Alabama by Monday afternoon, as a tropical storm. Their work may be closed for that day. We thought we were getting away from the storm and it's still coming to us in some form. Today we took the kids to a big museum in the area that was free. We all spent a few hours there. Lots of fun for us all.

Thanks Abigail for bringing us here. The kids had so much fun. For lunch we met our parents at a steak house. It was a relaxing day for us after all the driving.

VALLEJO FAMILY

Angela put a cross onto the front of their home for protection. They left their home at 2:30 a.m. The streets were empty. That's the best time to leave. They went to her mother in laws house in Miami. The 3 of them had slept there at her in laws home for a few hours and then they all got up to leave for Orlando. Angela, her sister, nephew, mother in law, Angela's husband, son Isaak, their dog, and their cat were all packed into one minivan.

The family left at noon towards Orlando and there was no traffic at all. They took I -4 and went with no problems. The family had 4 gas containers on the top of the van. They made it the whole way there on same tank. They didn't make any stops until they got to the hotel at 7:00 p.m.

The families had two hotel rooms. It was like a condo, 2 bed 2 bath. It sat on a lake with really nice spacious rooms. The family all unloaded and hung out there for a while at the hotel. On the resort property they went bowling and had dinner. Angela was very scared about the storm coming and not knowing what will happen to the Keys. She was sure that the Keys would be wiped out and all we have worked for would be gone. Angela and her family all asked questions like, will school be there? Will friends come back home? Will there be homes left for anyone? What will it be like trying to go home? It was the talk of the whole day and night. Angela's neighbor called her from the Keys and told them that he's staying behind. She was very worried for him too. Later on, a cop came by her neighbor's house and told him he couldn't stay. The storm will be too dangerous. He had to go to a shelter nearby. Cops were checking every home for people trying to stay behind.

BEN AND KRISTEN

This morning Ben and Kristen had been approached by the older man, again, for another night. This man wasn't all the way there mentally. Ben and Kristen didn't want to be responsible for him if something was to happen during the storm. They turned him away and told him he had to go to a bus to evacuate. They gave him no choice to stay. The man had seemed very far out and confused. Ben helped him get to a bus to leave, where he would be safe away from here.

The storm isn't supposed to hit till Sunday. Come Friday afternoon, Ben asked Dave what he had for supplies. Ben and Kristen felt the need to ask since Dave is in their hands. Harry is the owner and he's not here now. He went home to Key Largo. Ben is in charge of the buildings and grounds at the motel. No one else is at the Sea Dell working, it's now their responsibility to keep people safe. Dave had a case of water. One of his dogs just had surgery from being attacked by a pit bull yesterday. Only one vet was open to assist his dog. All Dave had to eat were 30 power bars. Ben told Dave he could be a problem for the city later and he may be a rescue mission for someone. Dave said," I will be fine." Ben told him he will come by and check on him later since the storm won't be here till Sunday.

Ben and Kristen continued last minute things they needed to have done before Irma attacks the Keys.

SATURDAY SEPTEMBER 9, 2017

3:23 p.m. I look at the weather again. It shows Saturday into Sunday for Marathon getting 100 MPH winds and higher. The news is expecting worse conditions than we all expected. IRMA came a little earlier in time frame than we thought. She's already hovering the Keys now. Rain fall is 12-18 inches. Storm surge is up to 10-feet in Marathon area. My whole family has been on the laptops with their weather videos. Some of us were on the internet already seeing live footage posted from Key West. Todd and I were viewing live cams from certain places on Duvall street. Our weather apps on our phones kept us glued when we weren't at Gwen's house. At one point many of us in my family had a meltdown. We were all in tears and crying for our community. Life back home may not be the same. My sister and her husband tried not to think about it. Todd and I were glued mostly to the storm. My sister held back tears about her home. She is on the water and is in fear for what they'll return too. I was crying too for all of our friend's homes and our work places. The kids asked me again if their school will be okay and their friends. I told them I hope it will all be fine. I made a few calls to Angela to see how she was doing. She was in fear too, as her home is ground level. We were all crying and not wanting to think of the aftermath we may go home too. It was a fearful day in worry and questions that didn't stop coming to our mind. It was a hard day for us. All of us stayed glued to the storm watching the destruction happen.

My mom, sister, the kids, Gwen, Abigail, myself, and Jose all went to a store nearby to go clothes shopping. Gwen and Abigail invited us to come to their church in the a.m. We didn't bring any dresses. We don't have to wear fancy clothes but our girls love to wear dresses to church. A little flea market store was in town for the week so we went there and found cute dresses for the girls. Megan bought warmer clothes for Riley and Beckham.

Later on that night we see cameras click out of Duvall street. Not soon after, all the cameras in the Keys were out, even the traffic cams. That's when we got startled even more. It's real. It was hard for us all to sleep that night.

VALLEJO FAMILY

All the food from Publix that Angela bought back in the Keys, were in the van. She left some can goods back at home and took the rest to their hotel. Her family went to Publix there in Orlando to stock up a little more. They went for walks around the lake just to get out before Irma came. The kitchenette made it easy to create meals and save money. They made lunch there, served steaks, chicken, and other fixings. The kids had mac and cheese. After dinner, they all relaxed, and watched some TV. "It's coming, we need to pray for our friends and town" quoted Angela. They all got together and did prayer over the storm. Angela, later, cried a lot feeling helpless knowing there's nothing she could do. She felt all they had worked for was going to be taken away. All her memories will be washed away. Angela said, "It is a feeling I never want to feel again. A very scary feeling. I am trying to be happy and normal for the kids, but it's hard to not let them see our fear."

She couldn't sleep. She Kept waking up and checking the TV news in hopes the track would move but it wouldn't change. It Just kept coming closer to the Keys. Angela says, "I was sitting in my hotel room in tears, as I remember things I had left behind. I was in fear of losing some personal items from family members that were personal made gifts or heirlooms. I was afraid of losing it all and picturing my home being wiped out. I've always feared for having a home in the Keys for this reason, it's all so scary. It's all okay in the house today and right now. Tomorrow everything could be all gone. I was feeling regretful and angry at myself for complaining about living in the Keys far from family."

She was thinking of everyone in the Keys and praying for those that stayed. She was worried for all the kids in Marathon, schools, and all their friends. Angela worried about everything and everybody." Courtney had called me when she had reached Alabama. She had told me she was safe and staying with friends there. I told her we were safe here with my family in Orlando. We both talked about home. We were worried for the after math of our friendships and homes that we have so close in the keys. We were all in fear for the same thing. All our friends and neighbors were all spread across the country for this storm" Stated Angela. It was a hard night for Angela to sleep.

BEN AND KRISTEN

This morning, near 9:00 a.m., the first wave came through of wind being near 65 MPH to 70 MPH. Irma was a day early. The wind was coming from the backside of the house. More of a NE direction. They were able to be on the porch of the home without being blown away. If they wanted to be outside, they moved their few chairs to the side of the house that had no wind. When the wind direction would change they would move their chairs to another part of the porch. They were dodging the winds. "We were thinking we still had another day to do things but we were wrong. You could see there was a rain break by 11:00 a.m. on the weather app. I wanted more ice" says Ben. Kristen had said, "No you aren't leaving." He said, "Oh yes I am. I will go check on Dave and then I'll be back."

Near 11:00 a.m. he drives to the Sea Dell to go to the big ice machine. They still had power. Ben took gallon bags and filled those bags up with ice.

Back at the house Kristen is freaking out. The trees are bending way too far for any one's comfort. Now she's alone thinking, "What if he doesn't make it back?" (in this interview Ben had responded to this question as… "You had a big gun." Her response to that was, "What would I do with it, kill a tree? "He responded, "Well you had protection.")

Meanwhile, at the motel, he filled up 10 bags of ice. He checked on Dave. Dave answered the door and said, "Wow you should try one of these power bars," as he was offering one to Ben. Ben told him "If this storm gets messy, I'm not inviting you, but if you feel your life is in Jeopardy then you need to call us so we can come get you so you can stay with us." They told him they had an extra bedroom for him and the dogs to stay in.

At the house Kristen receives a call from Harry, the motel owner, since she still had the motel phone in hand, she could answer it. He told her that the storm wasn't coming and she's fine to stay there; but in the meantime he actually evacuates from Key Largo. He was driving in his car while on the phone with Kristen and he was telling her that he is meeting someone in Orlando. Kristen was shocked about that. She feels really abandoned and wondered why her and Ben were left hanging to do it on their own. If it wasn't going to be a bad storm, then why is he leaving?

Ben arrives back at the house and Kristen wants to evacuate. She asks Ben, "Can we leave?" she had asked several times for them to head out. He replies, "It's a little late now, but yeah we could leave, but it doesn't make any sense. Where would we go now? We also have birds. We brought them to the beach house with us. We can't leave them behind. They wouldn't fit in the vehicle we had. We couldn't have all we need, us, and the birds in one vehicle. There is no room to figure it out last minute." She says, "Are you sure we just can't throw the birds, grab some things, and get the hell out now and dodge?" Ben says to her, "Kristen, we are so prepared, we are good for a month. Unless the roof blows off or the stilts give out, we will be fine. We are locked in now. We have to stay, and we are responsible for Dave in room number 1."

Later Saturday, the 2nd wave of the storm came through. It was worse than the first one. It cleared up again near 4:30 p.m. Ben tells Kristen, "Ok, we have another opening. I am going again to go check on Dave." She flips and says, "Oh no, you aren't leaving me here again on my own." He says, "The vehicle is under the house and it's still ok to drive. We have been watching the storm. If it stays the way it shows, then it will go away and it will get better. If it goes the other way in the north direction, then we are in for it and we will get nailed. I will wait these 45-minutes for the new update and see where the storm goes."

45-minutes later, it did hit that one area and Irma was sent directly North. Ben says, "Ok I need to take the truck to the top of the road and leave it up there so it doesn't get swamped out at ground level under the house. We have about a 30-minute window of opportunity to do things now." While this is happening Kristen and Ben start getting over-loaded with calls and texts from friends, her kids, and more family from all over the country saying, "Get out. Get out now. You can't stay."

Then Harry writes them "Just sit tight and you will be fine." Harry wasn't even in the Keys.

At 4:30 p.m. Ben went and parked the truck close to the road. Dave comes out of his room and says, "Dude, that last wave broke the awnings loose and it kept clinking against the window as if it's going to break through the room. The dogs ran into the bedroom, even the one with the stitches." Ben had told him to grab his things, the dogs, and come to the beach house. Ben told him he can't stay there at the motel. They arrive at the house. Ben and Kristen do not know this man personally at all. They are just trying to help him out. His two dogs were named Wally and Noodles. Ben and Kristen had taken the master bedroom already. They gave the master over to him and his dogs so they would have more space. Ben and Kristen moved over to a smaller room. By Dave being in the master bedroom he had direct access to the porch for the dogs. Ben and Kristen now have more access to all the house by being in the room near the middle of the house. They were satisfied with the new arrangement. Dave and Ben went to drop off Dave's truck to the top of the road. They parked it at the vet clinic. The manager had given them permission to do so days before. When they got back to the house Dave took all his items into the bedroom and got situated.

When the storm started to get worse, that's when the drinking started. The 3rd wave was the worse. No more driving. That's when they all introduced themselves to each other. Dave then noticed Kristen was the one who checked him in days ago.

It's 9:00 p.m. Saturday night. One of Dave's dogs had Downers. The dog had pills prescribed to him. It's to take pain away. The dog seemed a little out of it. Ben and Kristen had looked at Dave first thinking they were for him but they were for the dog. He re-assured them that he wasn't a druggy. Kristen and Dave went to bed early to try and sleep off their fear of the storm. Ben was on the couch late at night watching CNN. He said, "Oh man, I might have really screwed up. This is going to be really bad." Ben went to bed near midnight, on the couch. Usually 8:00 p.m. is a late night for Ben and Kristen.

SUNDAY SPETEMBER 10, 2017

9:19 a.m. Marathon High School posted a picture onto the internet showing the whole parking lot under water up to car doors. The high school became a last minute shelter for those who did stay behind. IRMA is still going strong onto the Keys. It'll be here tomorrow in Alabama as a tropical storm with lots of rain and 30 MPH winds.

We went to Church by 10:00 a.m. The kids went to their classes, while the adults headed for the church service. The pastor spoke of the storm and asked who was here from IRMA's path. Our family wasn't the only ones from Florida's evacuation. After church we went out to a fun taco place. There was nearly 15 of us. We took over 4 booths in the restaurant. That was a good place to eat.

Today we Celebrated Beckham's birthday. His party, as we mentioned before, was going to be a big party at club Duck Key in Duck Key FL., but the hurricane ruined it. We bought him a cake and let him have fun with it, as it was his first birthday today.

We stayed inside most of the day. Rain came in a little today but it wasn't from IRMA. Gwen's work called later tonight while we were playing games and canceled her shift. She doesn't have to work tomorrow because they'll be closed due to the tropical storm. Abigail still has to work because she will be on the later shift for Monday. The tropical storm is more of a morning shift issue for people here. By 4:00 p.m. there won't be much of anything except rain, according to the weather for tomorrow. The weather was clam for most of the day.

BACK IN THE KEYS

Hurricane IRMA status report – Sunday September 10, 6:30pm

A fellow city council member and mayor are with city manager and other first responders trying to get back to Marathon. They requested this message to be shared to all residents.

1. *The Keys are closed. Roads are in various stages of impassibility. Bridges, while possibly okay, will need to be inspected by DOT (Department of Transportation) before they are opened to residents. There has been a lot of damage done to structures and local infrastructure by both wind and water. There is substantial amount of marine debris from wrecked boats and docks in canals and local waters preventing access by water.*
2. *There is no power. There is no cell phone or internet services. Water may not be available. Communications and utilities are down.*
3. *There are only a few first responders in the Keys. They are stressed to the max with rescue and recovery efforts. They are prioritizing the opening of roads and the Marathon airport.*
4. *If there is a point to this message, it is this: DO NOT COME BACK TO THE KEYS UNTIL GIVEN THE OFFICIAL OKAY TO DO SO!! The city and county officials need to get the airport open to bring in needed supplies for those who are there and to evacuate those who need medical attention. Our first responders and essential personnel do not need any additional burdens as they try to do their jobs. STAY OUT OF THE KEYS TIL GIVEN THE WORD TO RETURN.*

VALLEJO FAMILY

Angela quotes, "The storms eye had just passed up near the higher part of Florida. The first report on Marathon came in at 6:30 pm to not enter the Keys until we are told to do so." Angela and her family were waiting for more words on the Keys and their home condition. They were glued to the TV all day, and on social media, trying to find any info they could on NOAA (National Oceanic and Atmospheric Administration). This site provided satellite home views of Marathon. There is no cell service in the Keys so you can't reach anyone there. Angela had said it was just a sad, scary day, waiting on what has happened in the Keys. She wondered, are people safe that stayed? Did people's homes make it? These are the questions that Angela's family and everyone else asked. They didn't find their home today as they weren't able to see their street available yet on NOAA. They plan to try again tomorrow. Today was a day of anxiety as they were waiting for more updates.

BEN AND KRISTEN

3:30 a.m. the house starts to move from underneath them. Ben was asleep on the couch. He woke up quickly as he felt the couch moving from its spot. Ben quickly turns on the TV to see what IRMA is doing. He says, "Yup, at least it's going a little bit west of us and we won't be nailed with a hit. Cudjoe Key, and Big Pine are right in the spot for the hit." Kristen and Dave slept in until 8:00 a.m. At that moment a huge gust of wind hit the house. Seconds later, Kristen and Dave, both busted out of the bedrooms simultaneously saying, "What the hell was that?" Ben replies, "That's IRMA just saying howdy." Kristen adds on, "Oh that's just great. She's the one that lifted my bed." Dave jumps in and says, "Is she gone? Is she just coming? Is she here? Has she passed yet? make her be gone." Ben continues, "Nope, she's still coming guys. This is nothing." Kristen recalls it being crazy. All of the wind lasted a little longer, so the 3 of them decided to go out to the porch, to chill and have a smoke. Kristen says, "I am never doing this again, never. I'm done. I'm never staying for another hurricane." They're all hanging by the door way to the porch. They start talking about hurricane Jose that was following out behind IRMA.

Minutes later Ben took a video of the storm, for their daughter, Bailey, and their friends. He captured footage with his phone near 8:30 in the morning while they were on the back porch. In the video he said, "We just got on the porch having a smoke while hanging onto the door knob so we don't blow into the freaking Bay." You can hear Kristen in the back ground saying, "Never again." Ben says, "It's a little scary, but I don't think we will be staying for the next one. If Jose's coming, we're leaving. Well if the roads still available. The eye is about another hour away. We are just getting the worst of it right now and for the next 2 hours. The house has been shaking since 3:30 this morning when Bailey called me. Hopefully this video will get to you guys. Alright party on. We will be drinking early today. Later." No one got this video. In that time frame it sounded like a monsoon of rain and winds blowing through a megaphone to extend the sounds. The winds were that strong. Some parts of it reflected the sound of a never ending tornado. Kristen stated, "Well if you can do IRMA, you can do any hurricane. Jose is just a category 3. There is no reason to leave. It's crazy."

The winds were a freight train moving at tremendous speeds you can't even imagine. Ben takes another video of the storm outside. Ben says," The eye has gone by. Oops Sorry Mcfalls family. Looks like you're going to need your fence replaced. Sharks are going to be swimming in the streets when this thing passes. Sharks are going to swim right through your fence opening." Kristen was for sure that storm surge was coming and that they would have to swim to get anywhere after the storm. As Ben was able to study the storm outside, he noticed that the worst parts are on the Atlantic Ocean side. The winds aren't moving in the direction to have storm surge on the Gulf side with them. The storm surge may miss them completely. Ben continues in his video saying, "Another 6 hours. Wait until you see that. This will all be flooded in here. Ok I'm going to send this other video to you guys. We're doing good. At least you can smoke on this side of the building." No one received this video. The video was too long to send it so no one ever got it. Both of them said that the storm surge never did happen to them on the Gulf side.

Seconds later, Noodles the little dog, walks out of the doorway past them. The winds picked her right up off the porch floor. Kristen quickly reacts and grabbed her. Kristen recalls, "I swear to GOD, this little dog would've been gone, if I had not reached out and grabbed her. She would've been blown away and been carried right off the balcony."

(Kristen tells me, during the interview, that the anxiety levels in the home were through the roof. She says, "No one knew if the roof was going to come off. Were any of the stilts going to give way? Because you could feel the whole house raise up under your feet. We didn't know if the sides of the home were going to snap in at any moment. None of us knew if the house would stay standing. What if the whole place just crumbled down onto us?")

"At 9:00 a.m. he takes another video. In it he says, "Okay, the eye has gone by Big Pine about a half an hour ago. Now we are on the shitty side of the storm and it's getting worse. It is hard to see from this video, but I'm telling you this coo coo cray cray. The house is shaking, now I was wrong though." In the middle of him talking, a huge gust of wind blows by him throwing him a little off balance as he says, "Oh wow, wow. We aren't going to get any storm surge because we are sitting on the back side of the eye. Ok talk to y'all later."

"The McFalls had a big 16-foot iron gate. All of a sudden, near noon, it just lifted off the hinges. It was chained to the wall side. It lifted up and then fell sideways. It was a good thing it was chained or it would've been gone. Those winds had to have been 160 MPH winds" quotes Kristen. Ben adds onto her, "The school clocked winds at 172 MPH." Kristen said she was watching the trees as if they were tied to rubber bands. She would see them sway completely bending in one direction and then snapping to a fall in the other direction. It was just one after the other with trees going down.

At noon they lost power, water, and everything. At this point they were just trying to stay alive. Everything was gone with nature. It was all brown and down. Then Irma left by 10:00 p.m.

IRMA DIDNT STOP US FROM CELEBRATING THE KIDS BIRTHDAYS DURING THE STORM.

BIRTHDAYS FOR ARIEL, LEONA, AND BECKHAM

BECKHAMS 1ST BIRTHDAY

HAPPENING IN THE KEYS

DAYS OF

ANXIETY

MONDAY SEPTEMBER 11, 2017

NEWS FOR THE KEYS

Monroe county will open re-entry into the Keys for residents and business owners in Key Largo, Tavernier, and Islamorada at 7 a.m. Tuesday. Entry require a yellow re-entry sticker or proof of residency or business ownership in those three cities. A road block will be put out around MM 74. The road has been washed out. An FDOT (Florida Department of Transportation) road crew will repair the road tomorrow.

Returning residents should consider that there are limited services. Most areas are still without power and water. Cell service is spotty. Most gas stations are still closed. Crews are still working to clear US1 as quickly as possible. All bridges have been inspected among US1. They have all been cleared safe to MM16. We are waiting for reports for the remaining bridges.

Crews will go house to house in the Florida Keys looking for people who need help. Destroyed roadways, isolating many who didn't evacuate when it slammed into the island chain Sunday morning. The eye of the storm landed in the middle of the Florida Keys. Labeled as a category 4 hurricane the swelling waterways came to an estimated 10-15 feet in some areas, reports CBS news correspondent Elaine. Water was lapping the steps of the Marathon High School, one of the few shelters in the keys.

One crew member from National Weather Service stayed behind in Key West to work with first responders. "we have been busy just trying to get information out there to people, to put them in the proper places to try and save their live." This one crew member believes the hardest hit areas will be between Big Coppit Key and Big Pine Key. Debris and a washout of the road isolated Big Pine from the other Keys.

One woman who stayed behind stated; "Irma has officially passed." She had stayed behind and rode out the storm. She said she was scared but was glad she didn't evacuate. "For those people who didn't evacuate they don't know when they're getting back in – it might be another two weeks, so now that we're here we can actually start to clean up, rebuild, and go from there."

First responders will be able to get out to the hard-to-reach areas today. The military will be flying in C-130 cargo planes to distribute water and supplies today in the lower Keys. The other logistical issue: authorities have asked people not to use their boats. The waters now contain too many dangerous pieces of debris to safely move around.

MY STORY

10:50 a.m. my family and I, see a picture of Marathon destroyed and underwater. This picture was an aerial view of the keys. We all go crazy online watching videos and looking at posts from others we know from the Keys. An employee from our work named Rocio, sends us a picture of a black Ford Explorer trapped in sand in the road way of US1. She had said that it looked like ours. She saw it on TV and snapped a picture of it to send to us. Jose responded back to her saying yes that's our Ford Explorer. She mentioned she saw it on CNN. This video went viral through our family, friends, and employees. We all saw it on CNN after she saw it. Then we saw our video on internet pages and video spots online. Our truck will be a loss. It probably won't be drivable again. It'll just be another vehicle pushed to the side by a larger truck.

Between us all, there were 3 laptops. All of us were engaged in the scenery on the pages we were viewing. As we were all seeing different things we were occupied by this mouth dropping situation. All the destruction, pictures, videos, and statements were all so unbelievable to comprehend.

Abigail and Gwen didn't have to work today, we were so glad Abigail was able to join us at the house. IRMAs storm is hittting us today as a tropical storm. Just wind and rain. It didn't become anything too major. It was a nice day for us all to stay indoors and play games. In between our games, we all kept checking the news updates in the Keys. I called my friend Angela to see if they're okay in Orlando. They didn't get much of the storm there. She does wish to know when we can re-enter into the Keys as we all do. Rumor has it that it could be two weeks before we can get back in.

Checking more videos and pictures we stumble across more clips of road blocks, boats, sheds, vehicles, appliances, furtniture, personal items, seagrass, and sand. It was all scattered across roads and properties. Items were just all over the place, as if they were rained down from the sky and fell in random places. I know someone who randomly received a trampoline in their back yard that was not theirs. My mom found a mango tree that planted itself in her yard (months later, May 2018, it was standing at 4-feet.) Later on we found out the other familes we know have been able to locate their homes online through some website. Some company is in the Keys taking pictures of every neighborhood from a helicopter view. Quickly we all start to search for our homes for a really long time. It Took a while to figure out how this was done. Familes and friends we know started posting, online, the condition of their homes. Everyones story was different. Some homes were missing. Other houses were destroyed, or damaged, or no destruction at all. We were all able to see peoples homes on the site that was being shared through everyone.

My mom was first to find their home. It was fine. Some shutteres were missing on the exterior. Megan and todds car was still there under the car port of the house with no surrounding water that we could see. They brought the other car with them. My mom has a camper in the back yard that had a plam tree fall on the roof caving a hole into it. That will be a total loss. Good thing they brought the boat while evacuating because it is new.

The rest of us were unable to locate our homes as they havent been posted yet. We will search them til they are on the site. As for the rest of the day it was just hectic with our hearts pounding in "What's next?" kind of questions.

VALLEJO FAMILY

Today they found the satellite view of their home. They saw a brown roof. "We are supposed to have a white roof" Angela said. Planes and helicopters had photos of the Keys neighborhoods. NOAA had screen shot their road and Angela had zoomed into the shot. Angela and her husband saw their roof was gone.

" Our roof had blown off. We were worried for storm surge. I was for sure that we had gotten ceiling and floor damage from the storm, especially now that the roof was gone. The storm had probably taken all our items out of the home. We were for sure it was all washed away "said Angela. Their minds were in a chaotic state of "What if's." They just wanted to get home as soon as possible to start addressing their home condition." It was a very scary feeling, but we kind of knew now what we needed to do next," quotes Angela.

BEN AND KRISTEN

This morning it was dead calm. Kristen tells, "I didn't want to go out of the house when I woke up. I was scared. Literally, everything was brown and down. Our porch thermometer got stuck at 105 degrees in the shade of the balcony. The needle reader got stuck after that. It was so hot. No air conditioning, electric, and no way to communicate with anyone". Later that morning the sky became a military fiasco. Ben said it felt like an apocalypse was happening. Kristen expresses, "The storm was kind of scary and exciting, but it's the days after that screw your head up." Kristen got physically sick after the storm.

No communication, no running water, nothing was there until Thursday. Today helicopters came low lying, house by house, asking people if they were ok. Ben and Kristen gave them the thumbs up so the helicopters kept traveling on. There were big military planes, with supplies, that were constantly flying in all directions above the keys. From 7:00 a.m. to Thursday, the military planes were constantly flying by every 15-minutes. Kristen was intimidated to leave the home. She didn't come out of the home until Wednesday morning. It was creepy going out at any time. Nothing was green. Days later when the Keys opened there was more green. Today not one palm tree had a green leaf that they could see. There is a little island across the water by this home. It was gone and leveled out. It was just a pile of brown on the island. It looked like a bomb went off.

They only had a battery fan to use for cooling off the 100 degree temperatures. The heat made you drip sweat all day. They had a battery radio to hear what's going on around them. The radio station, they were listening too, was 104.1 (US 1 Radio) it kept us alive. (Thank you Steve Miller, Bill Becker, and Ron Saunders) They had mentioned they were in the studio sweating it out. Someone had to be there so the local people could know what was going on. The radio station 104.1 had generators to help broadcast their station. Sheriff Rick Ramsey was driving to the radio station. On his way, he got a flat tire from debris on the road. He had to change his tire. Rick arrived to the radio station stating, on the air, "Don't go out if you don't have too. We are destroyed. This is the sheriff telling you to wait". Rick Ramsey got another flat after leaving the station.

While everyone else was out of the Keys, there had been so much clean up going on. You wouldn't even be able to imagine it. Kristen says, "I told Ben that he wasn't allowed to go to the motel, until there was some kind of M.A.S.H. unit for help". Ben states, "Fishermen's Hospital was destroyed. If you were to get hurt or cut yourself from Monday to Thursday morning, you were screwed. You better know how to stitch yourself. That's why she said you better not go to the motel. I told her I can stitch my left arm because I am right handed. But if I cut my other arm I am out of luck. I know She wouldn't stitch me."

Dave and the dogs turned out to be life saving for Ben and Kristen. Everyone took turns going down stairs to turn on the BBQ for cooking food. Ben was stocked on gas. He could cook meals for a month with his supply. They cooked coffee to make things seem normal. It was like camping. The dogs were comforting to them all. The one with stitches needed comforting. They were all so devastatingly hot. They took more videos of their surroundings. They were all there for each other. Dave cooked every meal. They all went to the motel later on. The Sea Dell motel was torn up. Kristen thought there was no way they could get it back up and running as it was. It was like their other home. They walked around the motel looking at all the damage.

Back at the ocean house... Iguanas, from all over, seemed to migrate to one island before the storm. Later today they all swam across the bay back over to land. The helicopters got low to see if they were sharks or people, swimming in the water. It was a massive amount of iguanas.

Monday night they remembered about the neighborhood cats that would hang near their home. Ben left the ocean house to go check on their home. Their home was sparred. Lots of yard damage. One huge tree in their yard, they thought would survive, didn't. This tree, super tall, fell right between their home and the neighbors. They were very lucky. Ben saw the cats had made it through. He fed them as he always did before the storm. He came daily to feed them. All the cats survived. They were shocked. Kristen didn't see her house until a week later. She wasn't ready to go home yet.

Ben expresses, "The worst part was seeing your area all brown like late autumn in Michigan". They are from Michigan. The air was still. The water was stirred up brown. Everything was brown".

TUESDAY SEPTEMBER 12, 2017

This morning Jose and I received an email from our landlord with a link to click on to see our apartment. It looked good from the ground level pictures we got. It was still standing 3-stories tall. The roof was still there. No busted windows that we could see. There was lots of debris all over the premises. I saw in the picture that many of the trees weren't there, while other trees were in pieces all around with their leaves and bark stripped off.

Few hours later my sister and her husband found their home from an aerial view. We were very surprised to see the roof and the home still there. Todd had to leave his motorcycle behind and somehow that was still in place where it was left in the back yard. They are one home away from an ocean front view of the water as their back yard. They live on the gulf side. With hurricane Irma coming in from the ocean side, the gulf side has been saved from damage. The whole family was so happy to hear all of our homes have been spotted and we all have a home to go back too. The interior is what we have to fear now. We don't know how much water damage Megan and Todd got inside. They are the only ones that are on ground level.

Minutes later my step brother, Richard, got a call from a family member in Miami. His mom and sister stayed there. They told him that his blazer got smashed by a tree in their yard. It's completely totaled. Richard parked it there hoping it would be safe. They did send a picture and that wasn't something he was happy to see. It was his only vehicle. Richard lives with my parents at their home. The one thing he has is the blazer. That was devastating news for him to hear.

After some relief about our homes we go to the local soccer field to play and run around. It's time to take a breather. While there at the park, my mom calls me to tell us they weren't able to get any hotel nights beyond the 14th on Thursday. All the surrounding hotels are booked up. Now we all need to think of where to relocate between now and then. Knowing we have two days to think on it, puts me in a panic. We don't know when the Keys will re-open. Great, what next? We finish our time at the park and I try to put this new issue to the side.

Later on we go back to the house and decide to leave the news off for the rest of the evening. We need to have fun with our friends. The guys went out for the night while us ladies stayed and played games for hours. This kept our mind off of the chaos for a while. Hopefully by tomorrow we will have a decision made on where to go next.

VALLEJO FAMILY

"Our other neighbor works as a fisherman and drove his boat to the Keys. He was able to see his home and checked on ours too. He had clarified that our roofs were gone. I still don't know the damage on the inside of our home with storm surge. I found out it will possibly be another two weeks before we can go back. I am completely livid and pissed that we have to wait. We want to get through the Keys so we can assess the damages on our roof." It had rained, Monday, after the storm and it damaged more items in the home that the Vallejo's could've saved if they could've gotten in earlier. They all left today, from Orlando, to come home to Miami and stay at her mother in laws house. Traffic was easy getting

WEDNESDAY SEPTEMBER 13, 2017

Today we celebrated Ariel and Leona's birthdays. Ariel is turning 8 on the 16th this Saturday and Leona will be 6 on October 21st. I always have their birthdays combined. Jose and I were going to take the girls to some fun places in Miami this week. The hurricane has messed those plans up for us. Today will be their day. I had done some research in this area and found a fun place. We are taking them to an indoor bounce arena. It's filled with many bounce houses and they have it all to themselves. Their own private party basically. All of us ladies, kids, and my husband, Jose, all go. The other guys were all sleeping and later doing other things. The bounce inflatables were loads of fun for us all. There were major slides, basketball bounce court, obstacle course, and more. Afterwards we took the girls to Chuckie E Cheeses. It was great. The girls won so many games and got loads of tickets for many prizes. We stayed there a while.

Later on we drove to a store to get the girls a cake. They pick it out and we got their names put on it. After the whole gang arrived at the house we then sang Happy Birthday. We had cake and more fun. Around 6:00 p.m. Abigail and Gwen had girl scouts to attend at their church. They teach classes. Ariel and Leona went with them since it was for their age. The girls wanted to go. They got to have more cake. Their birthday was celebrated there too.

While they were there, us other adults were glued to the TV and laptops for more Keys information. Nothing new on it. Just more cleaning up from crews down there along with inspections. Still no estimated time frame for re-entry. It's very annoying. It's hard to know where you will be in a week when you don't have enough info to point you in the right direction. Jose and I were looking up homes in this area of Montgomery Alabama. We were thinking we should move here. They are nice, cheap, and affordable. We can get jobs here. It's such a mess back in the Keys. How long will it be before the girls have to wait for school to start back again? We saw our place was fine but what about our jobs? None of the employees have heard any word on Lazy Days. All of us employees have been texting each other in a huge group text on what we know, and what we need to know. None of us know the condition of Lazy Days. Its driving us nuts. Many of us are wondering if we should move, look for new jobs, find other family or friends to live with, till we decide what to do. Being in this situation isn't helpful and its extremely frustrating not knowing anything yet on what to do. We are all on hold.

My family and I discuss where we are going to next. Gatlinburg Tennessee was in the conversation. Should we just go there and make more of a vacation out of this waiting game or do we try to go back? My mom and step dad make calls to Miami asking the situation there near Richards other family members. Miami seems to be doing alright. David calls Richards brother, David Jr., asking about his home situation. David Jr is my other step brother. He stayed in Kendall with some family. Jr is now back at his home in Homestead. Jr has 2 apartments open for us. He has 3 bedrooms in his apartment. The other apartment is his aunts. It also has 3 bedrooms. The arrangements were settled. Tomorrow morning, we all drive back to Homestead FL. to stay with my step brother. We will split up between the two apartments. Jr is staying in his aunt's place for now. The water pipe broke on the side of his apartment. He can't be there without water. The guys plan on fixing the pipe issue when they get there.

Jose and I decide not to do the late night drive again. That was too much. We plan to leave at 6:00 am and get a head start on the drive. Hopefully we will get to Homestead before dark. My other family members plan to sleep in and leave later near noon. Some are going out tonight one last time. Jose and I plan to go to sleep early.

The girls return from girl scouts. We all get ready for bed as we all have an early start in the morning. While saying our good byes to Gwen and Harry, we thank them for opening their home to us. Gwen tells us to wake her in the morning when we are about to leave so she can hug us one last time. Gwen, Harry, Abigail, and Aaron are all wonderful people to help us out by providing us a place to stay. It was so nice to see them all again.

VALLEJO FAMILY

Angela was still mad she couldn't get into the Keys. A good friend was nice enough to go to Angela's home and saw they had water damage and it all was damp inside. There were still a few inches of water in their home from the rain. They stayed in Miami and watched the news. There was minor damage at their mother-in-laws home. All of them in the family had to move trees and cut some down. They removed some debris from the yard. The house itself had no damage. That was a relief. Today was a cleaning day with family at her mother-in-laws house.

THURSDAY SEPTEMBER 14, 2017

We wake up at 5:45 a.m. Time to finish last minute packing and load up the car. In the back yard we grab our 3 large, filled to the top, gas cans for our ride home. In the living room, Rascal walks into his cage ready for the car ride. I take him in the carrier to the car. I sat him in the middle of the back seat and I go back inside the house. I walk to Gwen's bedroom door and knock. She and Harry come out once more to hug us all and say bye. We walk out of their house and head to our car for the long ride home. I had looked at my road app yesterday to check traffic in Florida and there were a lot of accidents. Tons of traffic almost the whole way through the state. I look at the app this morning. I see more traffic and collisions near Orlando and Miami area. It will be several hours before we get near there.

The weather is nice and cool out. It's really foggy this morning. It's been so much cooler here. I got to wear a jacket a few times. That was nice. It will be dreadfully hot when we get back home. Driving back towards Fl. was a pretty drive as we traveled through the country side of Alabama. The change of scenery was nice to experience over the beaches. One hour later we still had lots of fog covering the roads and trees. The roads were empty that we could see. Passing one gas station in the middle of nowhere, had bags on their pumps. We are still in Alabama. This wasn't a good sign of encouragement for our drive back so far. I find a new app while driving that was amazingly more helpful than any app I've had. This helped us the whole way back. It lets you know where cops are, detours, cars on road side, accidents, debris in road, lose animals near, speed limits, traffic ahead, traffic times to wait in it, and more. We would've been in trouble if we hadn't found this app. because it was very accurate. We were approaching the end of Alabama as we saw tons of military vehicles lined up on a road next to us. It was kind of scary to see that. Where were these vehicles going? Are the keys that bad? Do we really need this many military helpers back home? It was heart dropping to see. Is there some war about to happen that we aren't aware of? Later I found out that all those vehicles did go to the keys.

Yay we have entered Florida. The roads start getting messy pretty quick. Our alert goes off on the app about debris in the road less than one mile ahead. All the cars are going over 70 MPH sharing 4 lanes. We are on the lookout for debris and we slow down as we approach the apps location of it. Glad we had paid attention. It was a dinning chair in the middle of the 2nd and 3rd lane. We were in the lane to the far left so it wasn't in our lane at all. I can't believe there hasn't been an accident over that being there. The app was spot on for the location. That was crazy. So glad all the cars driving were paying attention.

About 30-minutes later our app alerts us again for more debris in the road. We slow down and continue with caution. It was a huge shopping cart laying on its side on the line of two lanes. How does something like that end up on this fast speeding freeway? Again no accidents. The cart was half way in our lane and we avoided it safely.

Two hours later our app goes off again for animals in the road ahead. I'm thinking this isn't accurate. How could there be animals in this road? Sure enough it was right again. There were four wild baby pigs browsing on their own on the road side. I've never seen that before. No accidents here either.

Later on there were so many accidents on this road all over the place like I've never imagined could be possible. I lost count of how many we encountered total. Our car was bumper to bumper traffic. This was worse than leaving Fl. We pass a bumper-to-bumper collision of two cars traveling too close to each other. After we pass that accident on the right side, there was still more traffic. We thought the traffic was from that one collision. Apparently the one we just saw had happened while waiting in this long line for the bigger one ahead. The big accident involved 3 cars that all somehow crashed into each other. 2 ambulances were at this one.

We were almost in 3 accidents ourselves in all this traffic and collisions happening all around us. Minutes later, at noon, I call my family to see where they are. They're just now leaving Alabama. They'll be there later tonight. They had lunch with Abigail, Gwen, and Aaron. I told them our arrival time is near 7:00 p.m.

We come across more accidents. All the cars had to move out of the way, again, to avoid hitting cars in front of them, and avoid being hit by cars from behind. I just wanted to get to Homestead. All this chaos was way too much. I was in a panic the whole rest of the way home. I prayed hard that we would make it to Jr's home in one piece.

8:00 p.m. we got lost trying to find our way to his home. Nothing was the same here. I didn't know where I was because so many streets were in pitch darkness. You had to shine your cell phone flash light onto some street signs to read them, because they were on the ground. Cell service for the direction apps were in and out. We finally made it to Jr's home in Homestead after running circles for 20-minutes. Walking into the apartment, we were given a bedroom and made our selves at home. Jose, the kids, and I shared a room for the night. Jr is in the other room till the water is fixed in his house. The 3rd bedroom, here, is empty with nothing in it. The girls will be in the room Jr is in by tomorrow when he goes back to his home. I walk rascal and let him stay loose in the apartment. Us 4 and Jr all go to dinner. We are all starving. We were thrilled to go to a buffet style dinner.

After dinner Jr. drove us around a little to show us more damage in the neighborhoods. It was a mess. The entrance to the keys was in the dark, and blocked off. Cops were directing traffic at the main light after coming off of the turnpike and before entering the keys. The power was out so no stop lights or street lights were working. It was pitch black. I didn't recognize this was the main intersection I use all the time when in Homestead. There were huge spotlights on this main 4-way stop intersection, with cones and cops all over blowing whistles at you when it's your turn to go. I assume this was an all-night thing for the cops for days. Some neighborhoods had full power while others, only a street over, were still in the dark. Some traffic lights blinked red for you to beware of the area in the dark. You could see trees down on cars, homes, yards, and streets. This is insane, and to think the keys are way worse than this. Back at the apartment we all are asleep by 10:00 p.m. none of my family has made it here yet. I call them to find out they're all driving separately. They'll arrive at different times tomorrow.

NEWS FROM THE KEYS

Update briefing from EOC (Emergency Operations Center)- Hurricane Irma Recovery

Key West – fuel, food, and water still needed in critically low supply in Key West. Military partners are bringing in large quantities by plane each day. Check point challenges - (one is at keys entry by homestead) is getting provisions through that are needed. Some trucks are being stopped. Grocery trucks, waste, and water trucks, home department trucks, and hardware trucks are being stopped in error.

Power – Keys Energy – ATT connectivity is high priority needed at the Keys Energy. Communications continues to be a significant challenge. 16% of power restoration stated at this briefing for Key West, Stock Island.

Sheriff- Law enforcement is in need for hotel rooms to house law enforcement. Needs for personnel to handle the check points. Reference to some angry residents ("Lots of angry people" who want re-entry)

attempting to re-enter the county. And the need for more personnel to handle the check point and to enforce laws in the county- reference to investigation/ enforcement against looting and other criminal activity. Difficulty of enforcing curfew in upper keys- more people in upper keys with power restored. Lots of people out at night and deputies can't stop each vehicle.   Consider to change curfew from 9 to 10 pm. all the law personnel are stressed. Lack of communication is the biggest problem- no phone, Lots of times creates frustration for lack of ability to communicate- especially with check points – suggestion- let all trucks through with supplies / provisions. No way for the checkpoint to communicate to verify who to let through or not. Satellite- cell phones are not reliable that have been ordered – lack of signal on the sat phones – "virtually useless". No successful lines of communication. Requests to private businesses not to sell alcohol.

FKAA (Florida Keys Aqueduct Authority) - some contractors are being turned away at the check point. This has been repeated. Engineers are coming in and are needed to make assessments and restore water. Water for Key West and Stock Island- from 10am – 1pm and 5pm – 8 pm. Higher flow is flowing down the pipeline. Power is restored to the stock to Stock Island plant. Crews are out on Big Pine Key and Cudjoe Key. Reports of people using water to wash cars in the upper keys. We need to clear message that water is for sanitation only for essential uses only. This is impacting ability to get water down to middle and lower keys. Everything is on a boil water notice throughout the keys. Valves at meters should be shut off if water is leaking at private properties.

HHS (Health and Human Services) Representative- Raised concern that allowing re-entry without providing bottled water is not advisable. Boil water notice in effect. Without bottled water is dangerous, as some folks will get sick from drinking the water being provided. (power is unavailable for most, so boiling water may not be an option).

FDOT (Florida Dept. of Trans) – permanent pavement repairs made at MM74. Other repairs ongoing. Final inspections of bridges being completed. Setting up debris sites today for removal, which is set for this weekend.

MCSB (Monroe County School Board) – school board- field space requests are being made for hurricane recovery efforts.

Marathon- reported Red Cross needs to create shelter plan. No current request made for people to re-enter. In need for a waste management plan. Debris removal from the roads are ongoing. Water pressure has improved over the last day. Still no power here.

Navy- recovery aerial tour conducted today with congressmen and other federal officers. Main priority is to push for water and food being transported by plane every day to key west. Boca Chica lodge requested to be used as a staging base for provisions/supplies. Full communication not established, waiting for ATT service.

Upper Keys – Power assessment ongoing. Food provisions are needed for emergency workers. Sanitation- waste management needs to have a plan to keep community safe and clean.

Re-entry to Key West and Lower Keys- No information provided this morning as to timeframes for re-entry for Middle Keys, Lower Keys, or Key West residents. No time frames are expected to be provided at this time. EOC (Emergency Operations Center) states that it could be a month or longer but would not commit to any time frame to allow re-entry.

EOC hotline/EOC E-Mail contact – no mention of hotline or E-Mail contact being Established for residents.

More info to come after 6:30pm EOC briefing to be posted later today Be safe.

A website will be established within next 24 hours by the EOC.

VALLEJO FAMILY

Today Angela took the kids out of the house. They did some local errands and helped with the home repairs.

Tonight Angela went to mass with her nephew, her son and her sister. They prayed for the Keys. She was looking for guidance on doing the right thing for her family. Should they stay or relocate from the Keys?

Tonight's curfew in the upper keys was dusk till dawn, according to the news. Marathon still doesn't have any updates on re-entry yet.

BEN AND KRISTEN

Today they re-opened the motel. They had 3 rooms now available with no power, or electric. Just a little bit of water trickled out of faucets. A family arrived at the motel office. This family said they don't care if there's no power, electric, or water. They just needed a roof over their heads. They had 2 pugs and 2 bulldogs with them. The family's home was local and it didn't make the storm.

Kristen leaves the motel shortly after with her golf cart. She and Ben were both surprised it was running. They didn't think that was possible. As Kristen appeared on 50th street a little man was standing on the side of the road. He appeared to be blind. His name is West and he is 80 years old. The man spoke to Kristen saying, "Can you help me?" Kristen replies back, "Sure, what's the matter?" He says, "My shutters are still on my window. My family won't come help me. It is so hot out." Kristen told him that her husband was right behind her. Ben got out and spoke with the man. Ben went to this old man's home and took the shutters off his windows and opened all the windows.

Later, back at the ocean front house, Kristen started making lots of food. She started feeding those nearby and walking up the streets to feed more people. People weren't prepared for the reality that happened. The community was in a shortage of food for themselves. It started feeling a little more normal with people nearby. Communication with others was a nice feeling. You didn't feel so alone anymore.

One of Bens friends, Nigel, had asked for some gas to run his home for electricity. Ben gave him 5-gallons of gas to help him out. Nigel had connections with the electric, cable, and water company. He got one man to come to the Sea Dell and hook up the electricity. Two of the buildings got up and running. Of course the one building, where the 2 pugs and 2 bull dogs were living, were in the building with no power. Ben ran an electric cord from one building to the other so this family could have air conditioning and a working fridge. They were able to use light in the room too. Still no phone communications yet.

West later came by their home asking for a banana and coffee. West would walk along way just to request a banana and coffee. This became a daily routine for him.

FRIDAY SEPTEMBER 15, 2017

At 4:00 a.m. I hear my cell phone ring. I pick it up. It was Megan and Todd. They were at the main gate entrance to get into the apartment complex. I quickly walked to Jr's room to wake him. I told him that Megan and Todd were at the gate and I don't know the code. Jr got up and called them on his cell and helped them get through the gate. Jr. waved them down as they approached the apartment number we were all at. There was no more room here at this apartment because the third room is not furnished. Jr walks them over to his apartment, which is the next building over. He got them situated in one of the furnished bedrooms. Todd and Megan would have to walk over to our apartment if they need to use the bathroom or in need of water usage. Jr comes back to the apartment I am in. Megan and Todd came over quietly to use the bathroom and get some water. I said hi to them as Jose and the girls are still asleep. I asked them where mom, David, and Richard were. They said they don't know. Apparently the family went separate ways to get here. Todd had heard that Richard drove over to a friend's home to stay and sleep at. No news on mom and David. Todd said he does know they're still on the road because they talked on the phone not that long ago. We all go to our rooms to go to sleep.

8:00 a.m. my cell rings again. Mom and David are at the gate. I wake Jr. again and tell him who is here now. He gets dressed and calls them. He helps them get through the complex. Jr. and I walk outside to wave them down. Mom and David follow us to the building next door, as they too, will be in Jr's apartment. I asked them what took so long and where their boat was at? David and mom had stopped by David's sisters home in Kendall to drop off the boat. They knew it wasn't going to be ok to have it here at Jr's place. Mom and David had been driving the whole night as well and are ready to fall asleep. Jr. shows them the main bedroom in his apartment for them to stay at. I say bye to mom and David as I leave for the other apartment. I wanted to go back to sleep.

I go into my room where my kids and Jose are sleeping and Ariel starts to wake up. I put on cartoons for her. I try to go back to sleep for another hour or so. I slept for about 40-minutes and both girls woke me up saying they're hungry. I wake up and get dressed and get them fed to start the day. Near 11:00 a.m. Jr. moves back into his main apartment and my girls take over the bedroom he was in. Both girls will be sharing that bedroom. It's a single day bed to share. They were happy to have their own space until we can get back home. The girls make themselves comfortable. They unpack their stuff and start to play. Everyone was up by 1:00 p.m. Richard shows up shortly after. Richard gets the empty room. David had a blow up for any family member that may need extra space to sleep. So Richard used the mattress for a night and then stayed with friends the rest of the time. All the guys went to a home store to get things to fix the water issue at Jr's place. Hours later it was fixed.

No info on the Keys re-entry. I've read on social media, from our towns webpage, that the keys may open tomorrow for MM 74 and below, while other resources still say it will be much longer. We are just waiting for the words to go back home. The main thing being said right now is "When the toilets flush then you can come back." Key Largo is opened for re-entry. José's family has gotten home already. They have a ground level home on the ocean side and luckily their home was sparred. No damage at all. We were all very surprised to hear that. It was great news. Key Largo has a few places open for direct needs. The grocery store is open and one gas station for sure. There may be more gas spots open. A lot of gas is for the volunteers and workers there. Us patrons have to be respectful on the gas. Curfew is in play for Key Largo at sundown. Cops don't want people loitering other people's homes.

My friend Angela calls me and tells me that her husband was able to get passed MM 74 as he is a government official. He has seen their home and the NOAA pictures were right. Their roof had blown off. Some of their roof, from the back porch, had landed in their front yard. Their home is flooded with inches of standing water. Alex is trying to get all the water out. He won't be able to get it all. He tried to find a way to cover up some of their items. Mold had already started to take over their home in the walls and ceilings. Angela didn't know what to do. She said he is spending the night down there in his car because he didn't have time to come back to Miami before the sundown curfew. She was freaking out as to what happens next. Does she go back or stay in Miami? Does Isaack start to enroll in school in Miami or go back to Marathon for school? No one has answers for any of this. All of us are in fear for what is next and the time frame of things. It's just a waiting game for now.

Later this evening we all played family games and had a big cook out with burgers. Tomorrow hopefully we will know something and have a re-entry time frame.

VALLEJO FAMILY

Alex leaves early in the morning for Marathon. He was able to get in before the public has re-entry because he works for the state. He drives to their home in marathon. He sees the damage. He called and cell service was very spotty. He said the roof had completely come off. Their Porch was in the front yard. Trees were down on the side of the house. The back yard tree was bare. Moss around the tree was still there. Inside the home it was wet. The mildew was so strong. Mold was already growing in the walls and ceilings. Alex tried to save what he could. It was very nasty in their home. Mopping water off the floor didn't help too much. The horrible smell outdoors was from left over storm debris and seagrass sitting in the sun. Coming into the Keys was unrecognizable all over the place. Cars, boats, sheds, items from homes, and resorts spread all over the road. Everything was all pushed to the side of the roads, like a bulldozer had come through moving snow out of the way. You weren't allowed to go pass MM 74 at this time, but he was allowed to pass that far south. It was like a bomb blew it all up. The scenery resembled winter but with hot weather. There was no shade anywhere.

"Courtney called me on Saturday. She was in Homestead with her step brother. She was in fear for her snake because she had left it behind in the home as she couldn't take her with them. I told her I'm sure she's ok. I told her my home conditions, where we are, and she did the same too" stated Angela. We both just wanted to be back home to get things back to the way they were.

BEN AND KRISTEN

Today there was phone service. It was a blessing when communications came back to their phone, but then it wasn't. They got bombarded, all at once, with texts from friends and family hoping they survived the storm. Kristen received 38 texts all from the 11th and Ben had received 48 texts. All the messages were comments of family freaked out for them. There was nothing they could've done to respond any sooner in regards to cell phones. Their phones went ringing today for the first time since last Saturday.

They went out to look for ice, due to all the ice being melted at the motel. It took an hour and a half to find no ice. You couldn't get onto the road because of the military, national guard, and the police. It looked like a war zone was going on. There were hundreds of military vehicles all over. When you did finally reach the road, there was no ice anywhere. They go back to the ocean house. Dave leaves on a hunt for ice. He comes back with 80 pounds of ice and 3 un-opened packs of Marlboro Red 100's in a box. Where did Dave get so much ice? There was a truck that had just pulled in and he just happened to be there at the right time. The truck helpers loaded him up. Ben says, "That's how it was every time. If you needed something, just send Dave. He always found a way to come back stocked. It was eerie. Whatever you needed he would go and get it."

At the motel all their rooms became available today. Every room was sold out by later today for the next 48 days in a row. There was no place to live. Locals all wanted rooms. On the radio, Rick Ramsey said he wanted to wait to let people in, later than tomorrow. Locals, at the start of the Keys, were mad. Every local wanted to be home. All those that evacuated have been away for 2 weeks. Everybody wanted to know if their homes survived and what the condition was. Not too many had money to keep staying away from the Keys. Ben thought that it would've been better to have people come back home after another 2-3 days later, as Rick Ramsey had mentioned. It was too much for the police to hold locals back anymore. Tomorrow the keys will be open.

Bobby, Ben's friend, came back from Atlanta Georgia with a bobcat being towed. The Sea Dell was his first stop. Bobby used the bobcat to clear the lot. Sea Dell was up and running full force by today. The past days, the owner wasn't there. Kristen says, "Without Ben and I, I don't know how the motel would've done. We poured our hearts into getting it back up. We wanted to make money again and have jobs for us and our co-workers. We wanted to help people like the locals, volunteers, police helpers and more. I can remember cleaning the rooms and I see a truck load of people pull up to the motel. They all jump out with chainsaws asking where to start. They were from a Mormon church. There was ten of them. 5 guys and 5 girls. They helped for a couple of hours and then the whole place was cleared out and ready to go. They were such a great help to us. They did amazing."

Most of the people who first got rooms were displaced people. The other people were gas workers from a company. They were supplying all the fuel to all the emergency first responders. They were great people. They took up 6 rooms. They were so nice. The gas company said to Ben they were surprised that Sea Dell had rooms open for them. The company was paying for all their nights in the hotel. Ben said, "You guys are the ones helping the Keys get back into shape." They were amazing.

The Cajun Navy had contacted Ben and Kristen. Days ago their daughter Bailey, from Sweden, was the last person they spoke too before all communication had cut out. They had told her they will be fine. 4-5 days later, she had contacted the Cajun Navy which was based out of another state. Their friends from Michigan were also in contact with Bailey to find out if Ben and Kristen were okay. Together they reached the Navy. Ben believed they were based out of Louisiana. The Navy actually had text Ben asking if he was alive and if they needed anything. They said they would send a helicopter to save them. The Navy told Ben that their friends from Michigan and their daughter, Bailey, had been trying to contact both of them. The Navy said, "They sent us to find you." Ben text back to the Navy,

BACK

TO

REALITY

SATURDAY SEPTEMBER 16, 2017

This morning near 6:30 a.m. I wake with a call from Angela letting me know that the keys are open for residents in 30-minutes and that we should hurry to the line. We are 2-minutes away from where the line starts so we think we are ok to wait a little longer. Todd comes knocking on our bedroom door minutes later about the keys opening and they're leaving in a few minutes. I quickly get dressed and rush over to the other apartment to see what is going on. My mom and sister are staying behind with the kids. All of us ladies are staying and all the guys are going back. There's no gas, cell service, or electric after Key Largo, so it is best the guys go. I refused to stay. Jose and I decided to go in our car. My step dad David, step brother Richard, and brother-in-law Todd, are all going together in David's truck. Jose and I say bye to the girls and we tell them we will be back a little before dark. I said Happy Birthday to Ariel, as today is her actual birthday, she turned 8. We all leave minutes after 7:00 a.m. with walkie-talkies to be able to reach other. The guys had 2 talkies and we had one. The walkies have a long range.

We were prepared for what was coming. We have our 3 jugs still filled with gas, packed our lunches, and drinks into a cooler. Food will be hard to find. Water is limited so we have jugs of water to do some cleaning at our home to conserve the water. The keys will be on a boil water notice for a long time I'm sure. We plan to check on our truck that's buried in sand, as we have seen in pictures. I hope to have our place cleaned out in less than 2 hours so we can be back. You can't be on the roads after sundown.

Driving over to Homesteads Walmart, we see the never ending long line of people trying to park. At Walmart we bought some cleaning items we didn't have back at home. After checking out we join the long line of cars and waited a bit to get to the keys entrance. At 8:00 a.m. we pass law enforcement as we enter into the keys. Our re-entry sticker allowed us to keep driving so we didn't have to show residency by driver's license. We drive along the 18-mile stretch of the everglades. It's much swampier now. In Key Largo we saw a few gas stations that were open. Mainly they were for workers and volunteers. Some stations had limits to how much you could pump at a time. Lots of traffic in the keys going south.

The Keys looked so eerie. The trees were all bare as if winter took over but under a summer desert heat. No green to be seen. No shade to hide from the heat. All the tree limbs looked like they were all clipped at the ends. It was jaw-dropping. Debris was all over the place. You could tell some big snowplow type truck came in and pushed all the mess to the side of the roads. The videos and pictures that were shown on social media and news didn't capture the reality of being there. My heart sank at every look of something destructive. There were mounds of seagrass, sands, and debris. Some sand mounds were so high they were taller than SUV's. It's so sad to see people's memories and items spread all over. Jose and I noticed scraps and furniture from businesses, restaurants, boats, homes, campers, cars and more.

As we enter into Tavernier, my step dad radios me on the walkie from Duck Key at their home. He said there isn't any cell service working in Marathon but their service is spotty on Duck Key. David says they do have electric on at their place. That's great for them. Mom and David's home have soaked carpets all through out, as their whole roof leaked. No open holes in the roof anywhere. Todd's car did encounter a high water level and it doesn't start at all. Lots of mildew and mold in their car. I'm sure their car will be totaled out. David mentioned that Todd is on the way to his place to see it and empty their fridge. We all forgot to empty the fridge. David said emptying his fridge was unbearable and so nasty. He was ready to hurl.

We approach Long Key and see our truck buried in feet of sand. So much sand that when we opened the truck door it was only inches from scrapping across the top of the sand to open the door. Looking inside the truck there was a lot of water damage. There was a water mark along our truck window inside. Lots of seagrass and coconuts stuck all around and under the truck. We headed back to our car. I noticed we had pulled over into a lot of sand. We try to back up onto the slight sandy hill and we start spinning tires. I start to panic because I had no bars to be able to call AAA. Jose told me to look around for a sturdy piece of debris to wedge under both back tires. We look around and found some wood pieces. We made sure to look for nails. These boards started to snap as we back up. We needed something more. We found some good solid rocks and metal sheets and we were able to roll on out easily. We move the debris back on the road side and take off for our apartment. We know now to stay clear of any sand.

Pulling into our place we see that it's been transformed by Irma. It is so hot out. it was in the High 90's but felt like over 100. No breeze so this made it way worse. No shade from our trees anymore so the sun cooked right onto your skin. No place to shelter from the sun except indoors. Our elevator is obviously out of service. We unlock our side door to the building. As we were about to walk in, I looked down and found a page from some one's photo album. This is sad. Someone's memories are shattered. Who knows how far along this drifted from the actual home. We step into the door way and could see the water line right away. It came up to my knees in the bottom stairwell. Wow that's a lot of water considering our place sits right in the middle of this island. Our apartment has views of both oceans. One half mile from Gulf side and Atlantic side. Jose's punching bag was sitting on the floor and black mold already took that over. That will have to go. The girl's bikes sat in the water but they're still rideable. we walk up to the 3rd floor. No damage to our place on the outside or inside. We were sparred. Only few people can say their place wasn't touched. The elevator is the only costly damage I have seen for our place. When we got into our apartment we moved all of our furniture back to its original places. We opened all the windows because it was so hot in there with no electric on. There was no breeze outside so this didn't help any at all. Our plants survived not being watered. We placed them onto the back porch to water them. Outside you could hear all the noises of trucks messing with the wires strung from home to home. Drills going into the ground. Electricians all over. It was just noisy. Screeching sounds from saws and tree cutters. It was insane. People all over working. It's like a bomb went off here.

All of our fish made it. We fed them. Our snake Layla was alive. Poor girl I'm sure she is starving for a rat. I then remember right before the storm we had just bought 25 frozen rats. They aren't frozen anymore. I'm sure they are all covered in maggots and nasty slime juice in the freezer. It makes me gag thinking about it. Jose said he wasn't touching the fridge or freezer. I opened it and it was hard to breathe. I had to hold my breath. I push everything into a trash bag. All the rats were previously individually packaged into sandwich bags. Each one was brown and bloated like a gravy balloon. Just one little pinch would pop that bag all over. I picked up each one and threw them into the trash bag. It was so nasty. I was right about the nasty brown slime juice. I was glad to see no maggots. I cleared out the whole fridge. I had to wrap up the trash bag into a few trash bags. No one knew when trash men were going to come through here so we had to wrap the bags well. I used so much bleach and Clorox in the fridge that it burned my eyes like cutting onions does. I had to walk away till I could re-open my eyes again. Jose was trying not to throw up the whole time from the smell. It made our whole place smell bad. We completed cleaning our place in 2 hours. We were so hot from being in the apartment. We went to our sink and splashed our face and hair with water. We knew not drink it. We were dripping with sweat. The water felt nice to cool us off. It was unreal how hot it was.

Jose wanted to check in on Lazy Days to see how they were doing. We drive by and park near the top of 11th street. The rest of the street was blocked by chairs and surfboards. We park the car and walk to the entrance. It was a mess of debris all in the front yard and by the front doors. So much seagrass and trash all over. The smell in the keys right now would be described as: dry seagrass, standing muddy water, trash, food, furniture, items, molded things, all cooking under the sun and mosquitos flying all around. Take that aroma and inhale it. That's how bad it was. This smell lingered for weeks. It was so bad at my place you needed a cover-up for your nose just to breath without needing to be sick. Adding humidity in with this, made it worse. Think of this aroma above: blended with a sauna heat, of humidity. It was unbearable. It would make you ill.

We walk into Lazy Days. All the kitchen crew guys were pushing all the sand out. They were washing and spraying the sand off the floors. others helped scrape the sandy water out of the doors of the main indoor dining area. It looked like a beach. I was surprised to not see more damage done. Something got flown into our bar as it had crashed in at one section of it. The outdoor ceiling fans were blown off of one side of the outdoor seating area. Part of our wall by the outdoor bathroom came down. All of our sun shade screens and most of our plastic awnings, to protect from weather, were gone too. All the marina docks buckled up or had been destroyed to pieces. Our dock in front of Lazy Days, somehow had no damage and was fine. All marina boats in the water had sunk in their docked spots or had floated out to the ocean and were stranded. Marina boats that were on land, and lifted up high, had all leaned over like dominoes to one side. You could tell which way the wind had come.

Jose and I stayed to help them. I wasn't much help but he was able to grab a tool to start pushing all the sand out of the dining room. We stayed for about 30 minutes or so. While there, I did have a few bars for cell service. I was able to call my mom and the girls. Told them what we had seen here and that we will be leaving in a few minutes to go back. Mom had said that Todd had called and they had only inches of water and their home was saved inside. We were all surprised to hear that. They were only one house away from the ocean. Todd's bike was still there in the back where he had left it. He had emptied their fridge and it was bad. Not like ours, we had rats. Todd and Megan have electric in their home already. They are one mile away from me. One bridge connects our two areas together. We still have no electric on our side and they have it on their side. That's wild.

We say bye to the guys at Lazy Days. We tell them we will back when electric comes onto our place. Many of us employees have been texting each other in a large group text. Over 100 texts have been between us all. Everyone's been wanting to know if we have a work to come back to, when will it be open again, what is the damage, does anyone have pictures, and more. I was able to answer most of these for them. Some of the employees may not come back while others don't know what they're going to do. We are all puzzled by the outcome. All the pictures I took at work, I sent them out into the employee group text.

Jose and I back up the car to heads towards home. We reach the top of the street and notice a friend we saw at Lazy Days all the time. Ronnie Ashley was a regular at the bar. We stopped the car on the side to say hi to him. He had told us he had stayed behind for the storm. He was in a storage shelter right now for a place to stay as he lost his home in the storm. He took us across the street to the trailer park that sits at the road top, of Lazy Days. He walks us over to his home. The trailer home he had resided in, had tilted over to the side. Everything in the home was destroyed from debris and water. His home is totaled. Jose and I walked over debris to look into his home and it was opened to his bedroom, as the wall was gone. It was clearly unsafe to try and step foot in there. You may fall through the floor or something may fall onto you. It was interesting to see his bike was still in front of his home. Irma moved all kinds of stuff but his bike still managed to stay on his little property.

We all 3 walk over to the house next to him. The foundation of cement blocks was there but no trailer. Where is the home at? I look over to the right side and there it was in someone else's yard. This home was literally sitting on the water and Irma's winds sent this home straight forward across the road in between two homes. This damage was bizarre. Ronnie walked us around the other side of the trailer park to see one trailer had been torn into shreds. Some of this home was sitting in the trees along US 1. There was nothing left to try and make anything of it. A woman and her daughter had just moved out of this home weeks before Irma came. Good thing no one was living in that home. There was seriously nothing left. It was tornado damage.

Jose and I thanked him for walking us around to show us what happened in here. All the homes had some type of destruction. Not one of them was left untouched. It made us smile to see he was ok. A few other bar regulars, we have at Lazy Days, also had homes in the trailer park. We saw some of them and said hi. It felt good to see familiar faces back in our town.

Once we made it back to Tavernier I call mom and the girls. Mom tells me the girls are waiting for us to get there. Mom says that her and David plan to go back home tomorrow to start working on their home and the outdoors. She also mentions that the guys are almost in Homestead. Todd and Megan also plan to go back tomorrow. We plan to stay in homestead until we have electric at our place and the toilets are safer to flush. The county keeps saying that some people are having sewage backing up into their homes from the wastes being flushed. The pipes aren't ready for all of this yet.

We arrive back to Homestead by sundown. Just in time. Jose and I played games with Ariel and Leona in our apartment spot. We made the girls dinner as well. They asked when they get to go home and I told them we have to wait a little longer. They were sad. The others in our family get to leave tomorrow and we are waiting. When it came to bed, the girls went to the room and started to cry about sharing a single bed again for another night. They wanted to go back home. They missed home and their beds. Poor Leona missed home so much she claimed to forget what her room looked like. She's funny. They were sad. They didn't like having to go to bed in the dark again in a new atmosphere. It was fun for the first 2 nights but now it isn't fun for them anymore. I told them we will go home as soon as we can. I told them I loved them and I will see them in the morning.

VALLEJO FAMILY

Angela's husband stayed overnight last night in his car. It had rained so much during the night; it woke him up. He had mopped the floor a 2nd time earlier that evening and now the rain was coming back into the home, through the roof. He tried to put towels down to help but nothing was helping.

There was nothing he could do to stop the rain from coming in a 3rd time and causing more damage. He leaves mid-day from Marathon to go back to Miami.

He arrived to Angela and Isaak. Angela asked him, "Do we go back home? Do we move somewhere else? Do we enroll Isaak to school here in Miami with my nephew and stay here? We don't know the condition of his school or when it'll restart again." They went to the Hollywood Florida Home Depot for tarps for their homes roof. Family members gave them tarps to help as well. Angela had a sense of relief knowing her husband went already to their home and has seen the damages. They now know what they need to rebuild. She told her husband they have to go back home. Angela said, "We can't take our son away from his friends and school. When the school opens he will be there in Marathon. We will not be separated due to this storm. We will stay together as a family close by, and we will do what it takes to make this work and rebuild." She decided she didn't want to change their life due to a storm. It wasn't going to make her give up.

Angela had left Isaak with her sister hours later, and she joined her husband in going to the keys. "The drive through the keys was very sad to see. Everything was all over and ruined. Dead trees were all over the area. Resorts had all been devastated." She was very much in shock." It was very sad to see this in our town."

Angela's reaction to her home on the outside pulling up – "I was crying and balling out in tears. I couldn't understand how the house was still standing, but the roof was gone. The surrounding homes roofs were fine. We found out, later, that a tornado went right over our home. 4 homes, including ours, all lost roofs. They were all in a perfect line from tornado winds."

Angela's reaction to the inside of her home – "Complete aww struck. It smelled so bad. It was overwhelming and sadness to how we could ever fix this. I felt fear. It didn't feel like home at all. Such sadness to wish I could've done more. Thankful that our friends we spoken with were all safe. We had great neighbors that helped us out putting a tarp on our home. Our neighbor that had stayed behind, had helped us so much with the tarps, cutting down trees, and moving debris from the yard. The home of the couple next to us, also chipped in to help us out. We helped them as much as we could too. All of us helped each other. The ones with less damage or no damage, had helped us a lot. My husband and I had stayed 3 nights here, in a room, on our futon, that made it through the storm."

Publix was open. They were able to cook. Power had come on today. The two of them cooked outdoors on the grill because they couldn't use the kitchen.

THESE SCENES
STRETCH
FROM LONG KEY
TO
BIG PINE KEY

OUR EXPLORER

CAMPGROUND BELOW

CURFEW
DUSK TO
DAWN

BK DRIVE-THRU

TOP OF 11ST NEAR LAZY DAYS

Ronnies home was totaled

ABOVE: RONNIES HOME WAS TITLED TO THE RIGHT SIDE . HIS BIKE STILL MANAGED TO STAY WITH HIS HOME. RONNIES HOME WAS ONE HOUSE AWAY FROM THE HOME BELOW

mobile home was here

Now mobile home is in the road

CANAL PHOTO

MONDAY SEPTEMBER 18, 2017

Yesterday on the 17th all my family just hung around for another day in Miami. We all mostly spoke of when we should return home to stay and what to expect by leaving for home before all necessities are back to normal. My family said they'll just leave Monday.

This morning, on the 18th, my mom calls me around 8:00 a.m. and tells me they're packing up right now to leave and head home within the next hour. They have electric and running water at home. They're going to start cleaning up.

Megan and Todd call us minutes later to give us the heads up that they are loading everything up into their car to head home as well. They too have electric and water. They want to get back on track of normalcy.

People's homes are getting backed up with sewage from toilets being flushed. The water is under a boil water notice until otherwise stated. We are waiting until at least the toilets are safe to flush. We also need electric back before we go home.

Once all the family left we had the day to ourselves. We just hung around the apartment and later found a park to play at till dark. Later on that night I received an email from my landlord that our electric is ready to go and they'll turn it on once we get there. Jose and I decide that we will go back home tomorrow to stay. The girls were so excited when we told them. When we got back to the apartment the girls packed up all their things so fast in excitement to go back home to their rooms. They haven't been home since the 6th. We call our families and tell them we are coming home tomorrow morning. Jose and I pack up the car so we can head home near sun up. We want to beat others trying to enter back into the Keys. The girls had issues falling asleep because they were so happy to be going home.

BEN & KRISTEN

WE ALL MET
AT LAZY DAYS

SEA DELL MOTEL
the sign blew off

THE MOTEL ENTRANCE
WITH TREES IN THE
WAY

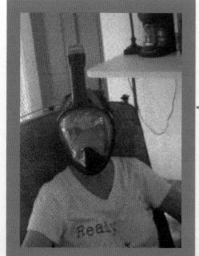

THE SMELL WAS SO HORRIFIC
THAT IT WAS HARMFUL TO BREATHE
IT IN. MADE YOU SICK TO SMELL IT

THEIR BACK YARD
IS DESTROYED

TUESDAY SEPTEMBER 19, 2017

At 7:00 a.m. Jose and I woke up to get ready and then got the girls up. They stayed in their pajamas. We looked around to make sure we got everything. Looking in the fridge, we decided to grab all our food and load it into our coolers. We were all in the car within 20-minutes. We couldn't wait to get home. On our way out of the apartment complex my mom calls me and says that our Publix and Walgreens are back in business already. Yay that's great news.

Jose drives to go get ice at a nearby gas station and fill up the car. Pulling out from the gas station we could see the start of the re-entry line to the keys. Not a long line at all. We entered through re-entry with no problems. 20-minutes later we arrive to Key Largo. This was Ariel and Leona's first time seeing the Keys since the hurricane hit. They were sad for all the people who lost their items, cars, boats, home furnishings, business belongings, and personal items. It was an eye-opener for them. They were spotting toys, kid bikes, and more along the piles of debris. The girls couldn't believe all the mess they were seeing. The trees had no leaves and they were all bare. Both girls made comments about being sad for all the trees. Nature lost its life and were skinned bare by Irma. The girls asked questions most of the way home and were awing about everything they were spotting. It was weird for us all to see the Keys being so different.

Once we arrived in Marathon, we saw many signs all over of "Volunteers here for you." People came from all over the country to help the Keys. We saw many signs for "Baby items and moms," "Hot free meals," "Free food and water," "Water and ice," "Necessities and toiletries," we saw it all. It was very moving to see so much help here already. We arrive at our apartment and somehow the elevator was working. All of us took our bags, pillows, blankets, and more all in one trip up to the third floor. So glad that was working. When we got inside, it was dreadfully hot. So hard to breathe in the hot air that still smelled so bad from the terrible fridge. It was gagging air to breathe in. I call our landlord and tell her we are here. Minutes later she sent our maintenance guy up. He quickly inspected our place and then turned on the electric. Once it was turned on, we set our AC to really cold. We have hopes that the cold air will take away the smell in the apartment. None of us unpack our things. Our top priority was to get out.

At 11:00 a.m. we got in the car and turned on the AC. We scrolled through Marathon's social media to see where some certain spots were. People had posted about the high school being helpful. We drive over to the school. Military men in uniform were there with just MREs left. They had no more packs of water. They told us we could drive to Marathon Community Park, as they had water packs there. We didn't choose to take any MREs. As we finished pulling around the drive way of the high school, there were more military men in front of an 18-wheeler handing out tons and tons of ice. One man handed us 2 large ice bags and offered us to take as many as needed. 2 was good for us. The food truck at the exit was packing up to leave. Their last meals just went out to the car in front of us. There wasn't any for us. The ice guy told us that we could also get food at the Marathon Park.

All 4 of us drive over to Marathon Park to see what they had. There was no line at all as we pulled in next to the skate park. There were volunteers and military personnel's there. They asked us how many people were in our family? There is 4 of us so we were given 4-24 packs of water. It was so awesome to receive that much for free. Next they also had MREs but we didn't need them. We pull towards the exit and see another food truck labeled "Salvation Army". Jose parks the car and I walk up to the truck. So glad to see people were there and they had food. They made me 4 containers of food. In each to go box was green beans, pot roast, and peaches. This food truck had served 150 people today in Marathon. Yesterday in Key West, their other food truck fed over 1,200 people. Wow! The food workers had many trucks in the Keys from New York, Massachusetts, Maryland and middle FL. I thanked them for contributing their time and helping our community. They said they are here until they're no longer needed.

We drive next door to the American Legion building. They had a lot of free supplies, food, clothes, baby items, water, and more. I ran in quickly and grabbed a few bags of food to hold us over until our fridge is cold again to hold groceries. We head home to eat as we were so hungry and tired of sandwiches from our packed food coolers in the car.

Once home we all got situated in the house. It felt so much cooler inside. The smell still lingered. I lit many candles and sprayed a lot to rid of the smell. The terrible scent was still there but not as bad. We all sat down to eat. We opened the boxes and there was so much food in each one. We were able to save 2 boxes for tonight's dinner. All of us got full from two boxes. The food was so good. We used the water bottles for drinking. We boiled tap water over 2-minutes if we needed it for any cooking. We used the water bottles for brushing our teeth at night as well. The girls knew they had to stay away from tap water. When it came to bath time and showers they knew not to allow the water to enter their mouth. The boil water notice was in effect until further notice, who knows how long.

Later I got a notice online from the elementary school's page stating that school won't be starting Monday the 25th. Instead school will resume Wednesday the 27th. By then all toilets, septic tanks, and water should all be fully safe to use again.

Still no cable, internet, or home phone lines working. Only cell towers are working right now. My kids are super bored. We have played every board game repeatedly, and have gotten tired of coloring in coloring books. None of the playgrounds are safe to play on yet. I haven't heard that any are opened as of right now because they all have suffered damage. Most of the playgrounds have fallen trees on them.

Our fridge will be smelling bad for a while. Its near 8:00 p.m. now and the smell is so unbearable. We will have to wait a while before adding food. Each time we open the fridge or the freezer it re-sends its terrible scent back through the house all over again. If food was to go into the fridge it would soak all the smell up and it would make you want to throw up. It makes me gag every time I have to inhale that bad smell. This smell in our fridge lingered for another month and a half before it was mainly gone. We had to wrap up food way better than we ever did before just so the scent wouldn't get into our food and contaminate it and taste like the smell. We used so much bleach, and baking soda in the freezer and fridge, it was insane.

Outside the smell is still so mind boggling. I walked my dog near 7:00 p.m. and I couldn't breathe as I walked him around my building. I had to have a shirt covering my mouth. It was like trying to avoid breathing in deadly fumes. Picture this: sun beating on you through the bare tree limbs with no shade, and the sun beats onto your skin like fire. Sun rays feel like 105 degrees when its only 97. Your body quickly starts sweating and dripping with no breeze around. It's like walking in a desert. Everything is still. Next to you and below your feet is welted sea grass, blended trash, molded blankets, furnishings with molded material coverings, all sitting in still water. The water has mosquitos, algae, and mold from all the trash debris. Now cook all of this under the sun for days and days. Let's see how long it takes you to throw up or gag. It's so nasty to walk by this 3x a day to walk my dog. It is like this everywhere. Some spots are worse than others. The heat just makes it unbearable. All the debris has become spoiled. it's such a killer. It's depressing. News cannot capture the smell that we inhaled.

Jose was gone most of the day helping Lazy Days get cleaned up to re-open in the next few days. We need our jobs. Being broke, not knowing when you will have work, and money again is frightening. Everyone is in fear for this same issue. Many people don't know what to do right now. Only thing we can do is help each other to get things back to normal as much as possible. We were all in bed by 10:00 p.m.

VALLEJO FAMILY

Angela and her husband went back to Miami later, on Tuesday, to see Isaak. Her husband's coworker was kind, and offered to let them stay in a hotel by a local restaurant in Marathon. They took the offer. They took their dog and left their cat behind in Miami. All 3 of them left Miami tonight for Marathon and stayed there in the hotel for a couple of nights.

AMERICAN LEGION WAS OPEN RIGHT AWAY FOR ANYONE TO GET DAILY NEEDS

THE VALLEJOS COME HOME

BURGER KING IS A MESS

This was a 3 story complex that crumbled down to 1 level

ALONG US 1

THEIR ROOF ENDED UP IN THEIR DRIVE WAY, ALONG WITH THEIR BACK PORCH

VALLEJOS BACK PORCH WAS BLOWN AWAY

EVERY LANE OF TRAFFIC MOVING 5-10 MPH ENTERING THE KEYS FROM HOMESTEAD

WEDNESDAY SEPTEMBER 20, 2017

Jose goes to Lazy Days to help them get open soon. The girls and I stayed home being bored. I am glad that we did have a VCR and movies to watch at the house. We watched a lot of them. We were happy to have our home and items still here. As we have driven around and seen so much loss and destruction it was sad for us all to witness it. I call Angela and she tells me that their home is not livable. She and I have been in touch through this whole journey so far. She said she has a friend that will be lending them a camper for them to stay in until their home is fixed. That was great to hear.

Jose calls me near 3:00 p.m. and tells me he got electrocuted. I freak and tell him to go to the hospital but he refuses. He insisted he was fine. He was in the kitchen with flip flops on helping to rid the water out. The electrical cord from the ice cream cooler was laying in the water in a hidden area. None of the kitchen crew saw the cord. There was no electric on yet for the restaurant. Near 2:30 p.m. it was turned on without notice. Jose was standing in the water when the power was turned on. The electric shock was so strong it knocked him to the floor. He was laying in the water feeling electric shock through his whole body. He crawled out of the water while being electrocuted and jolted around. I monitored him for days. Thank the lord he was okay and never needed a doctor.

Social media posted "Curfew here in Marathon has been changed from sundown to now 8:00 p.m."

While walking my dog near 6:00 p.m. the girls came out riding their scooters. We walked our dog by Burger King which is next door to our building. As we walked around we found items in all the debris. Leona found a little basket and started making a Lego collection in it. Each time we went out to walk the dog and both girls would look for more Legos. We would soak the Legos in bleach and water. We scrubbed the basket clean of all the nasty seagrass and germs that accumulated onto it. Now they have fun walking the dog. They started to ask when we could walk him again. They called it a treasure hunt. Some one here in Marathon had a nice Lego Collection.

Later tonight near 10:00 p.m. I went to walk Rascal. It was very creepy. Many businesses around me were still in the dark. This road is usually well lit and bright like a football field. Tonight it was a spooky football field in the dark. Only a few emergency building lights were on. I had to use the flashlight app, on my cell phone, just to see while walking him. US 1 was dead with no movement of life, cars, lights, or anything. I was scared to be out walking him. My husband and I didn't think it would be this dark. I walked him as fast as possible. I had weird feelings around me in the dark like that. Everything was still and calm. Not even the wind was moving. Five minutes tops and I was back inside. I didn't walk him past dark anymore until power came back to all the businesses on this road and US 1.

Curfew for our area has now been bumped up to 10:00 p.m. This is nice to hear. At 9:30 a.m. Jose, the girls, and I all go to Lazy Days. All 4 of us are going to try and get the restaurant open for business in the next day or so. After being at work for an hour helping clean and put things away, our boss tells us "Hey, we are opening in 30-minutes." My response was speechless. Well I'll be staying here for a while with the girls. We aren't going home anytime soon. I am expecting it to be slow due to the storm, and none of us have money.

The owner has me write with spray paint, onto a piece of ply wood that we are now open. Quickly after this sign is out at the top of 11th street, people start walking in for lunch. We got way more people than we expected. We were working with a cash only base system. We had to hand write down all of it. Writing tickets was a challenge since we are spoiled with computers. On average we were writing 4 tickets per table: one for our self, one for the kitchen, one for the bar, one for the customers to see total, and an extra one if they wanted a receipt. It was crazy hard to do this when we got slammed. It was only my husband and I. He and I both were serving, bussing, running food out and bar tender all at the same time. The owner was helping us. Nothing in the kitchen was in its normal place. We had to run to the walk-in fridge to dish out each individual sauce needed. There weren't any working fridges in the spots where we usually have them. All the cold items were in one fridge. No ice was safe to consume. All ice to customers came from donated trucks of ice. All drinks were not from our soda machine, as we couldn't use it either. All sodas were poured from 2 liters. We had limited choices available. All water was from water bottles. We got customers a cup and some ice from the ice bag. It was chaotic and very time consuming to be running all over the kitchen, which is like a maze, to find items. We needed Ariel and Leona to help us out. We put them to work. The girls took condiments, refills, fries, and more little items to all the tables. The girls even made tips. The locals enjoyed seeing us as a family help out. The girls were hostesses too. They sat people down for the restaurant when they weren't running items to customers. People thought it was so cute when the girls asked how many people, if they wanted indoor or outdoor seating, and to follow them to the table. The girls made near $30 together this day. The girls and I stayed till 4:00 p.m. Another server was available to come in and take over so the girls and I could go home. Jose stayed to help out. People were extra generous on their tipping. We weren't expecting that at all but it was very much appreciated.

The girls and I went home to take care of Rascal and play until Jose was done. Near 9:00 p.m. I call Lazy Days and remind them of the curfew at 10:00 p.m. None of them, except Jose, knew about the curfew. Our owner and other employees at the time, both lived in Key Largo. The owner called the police station to double check. I was right and he quickly tells all employees to not worry about closing duties due to the curfew time, which is in one hour. They all told guests that curfew is shortly near. Everyone closed tabs and cleared out of there like there was a fire. At 9:45 p.m. I call Jose about him needing a ride. He was last to leave. Jose tells me that anyone can be arrested if seen out on the roads past 10:00 p.m. I flip out. I leave with girls at 9:50 p.m. to get there to him. It takes almost 10-minutes to get there too. The girls are scared thinking we will get arrested and taken to jail. They started to ask if kids can go to jail. I was re- assuring them that the police would probably let us go if they see we have kids and we are headed for home. At 10:00 p.m. I pick Jose up. He was the last one to leave. The others from Key Largo left minutes after the phone call, because they have a one-hour drive. Jose was waiting for us at the top of the street. He gets in the car and drives. We drive away from Lazy Days and passed 3 cops that had their lights on and flashing. It was our warning to get off the road. I assumed they gave people a 10-15-minute grace period to get off the roads. We made it home with no cop issues. All of us ran inside to our apartment. All of our hearts were racing so fast. Those 10-minutes were an adrenaline rush. We were happy to be home.

LAZY DAYS SOUTH

OUR SIGN BEFORE IRMA

OUR GIRLS HELPED OUT FOR ABOUT A WEEK TIL THEY WENT BACK TO SCHOOL

OUR SIGN AFTER IRMA

THE FRONT ENTRANCE WAS A DEBRIS DISASTER

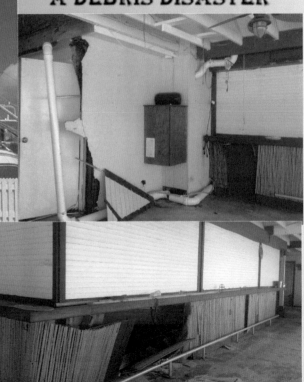

ALL BOATS AT THIS MARINA FELL TO THE SIDE LIKE DOMINOES

THE BAR AREA WAS DAMAGED

FRIDAY SEPTEMBER 22, 2017

Tonight the fire alarms in my apartment building go off near midnight. My whole family and I jump out of bed and run to the hallway to see what's going on. Everyone else came from their rooms too and no one had a fire. Jose and I, with the girls, all stand on the back porch while calling the fire department to come turn off the switch. 10-minutes later the fire truck arrives. My family stays on the back porch while a neighbor and I go down the stairs to talk with one of the men. We tell them there is no fire. They look around the premises and tell us that our garbage shoot has a lot of humidity and moisture in it. The censor is reacting to it as if there's a fire. The fireman was able to use his key to turn the alarm off. He said it could go off again but there is nothing they can do to make it not go off again. We have to tell our landlord tomorrow to get someone to fix it. These alarms are so loud. It screams in your ear over and over. It's so loud you can't hear any one talk to you. We all went back to our beds in fear of the alarm going off. It haunted us the whole night. Every few minutes I was jumping awake in fear of it going off again. I prayed that I could sleep and it would stay off. Thankfully it didn't go off again. I sent an email near 5:00 a.m. Saturday the 23rd to my landlord on the issue. Near 7:00 a.m. the alarms rang again. Glad we were awake. They went off again near noon. 2:00 p.m. rolls around and the alarms were fixed. Later I found out from a nearby neighbor, down the road, that the alarm here was going off for almost 24 hours on Sunday night the 17th. No one in the building was home, or working there for the alarm to be addressed. My poor neighbor said he had to go to sleep hearing it going off non-stop for hours and hours. Someone finally called it in. Someone must have come and turned it off. I couldn't imagine what it would be like hearing this alarm for hours. It killed me to hear it for a few minutes, and even when it wasn't ringing anymore, I could still hear it ringing in my ears.

VALLEJO FAMILY

A friend of Angela's husband was so kind to let them borrow their camper. The Vallejo's were able to move in that day to their front yard with it. They officially moved all their items into the camper on September 23rd. They thanked them so much for helping them. Cleaning and trying to make everything back to normal for Isaak, made it feel more like camping for him. Just trying to make things feel better for the situation. It was important to Angela that she gave safety rules to Isaak when he wanted to play outside, so he wouldn't get hurt with all the debris everywhere.

The family had gone to the Salvation Army Food Truck, at the park, for some meals. They also received plenty of water, as it's not safe to drink the water. Next they went to Publix for boxed food and can goods to stock up for a little while. Today was a busy day trying to get situated into their new living space. Their next few days was just adjusting on being home again but in a new temporary home.

SUNDAY SEPTEMBER 24, 2017

The girls and I worked Thursday and Friday with both days being super busy. I was given the day off on Saturday to be with the girls. Some more employees came back into town and were able to get back to work. We didn't do much on our day off except collect more Legos and play indoors.

This morning we got word that our elevator is back up and working again yay. Today we needed to go back to work. The girls came with me. We are working 10-4 p.m. I got the girls dressed in our uniform shirts for work. I got them each a small size and twisted one end up into a pony tail band and hid that part under one corner of their shirt. Now the shirts looked like they fit them. They were ready to work now. Today the water was safe to drink again. This saved us a lot of time. No need for ice bags, 2 liters, water bottles, pre boiling water, it's all a relief. Today was another busy day of running around and making money. The girls made more money today too.

We walk Rascal so we can go Lego searching some more. The girls grab their scooter and a blue grocery bag to put the Legos into (this is the picture on my front book cover). Today while walking the dog I came across a blue lunch box that had a name and phone number on it. It said "Waldera." This must be the families last name. it's a crucial time for us all. I know if I could have someone return anything that I've lost in this hurricane it would be like receiving an award. I call the number on the lunch box and Mrs.Waldera answered the phone and was very shocked that anything was found. She had said her home burned down in the midst of the storm. She didn't think anything would have survived the storm. She had guessed that the lunch box must have drifted before the fire happened. I told her where I lived. She was from the Ocean side. She lived in a neighborhood across the street from where I was. She mentioned that her son (Cameron) had lost a Lego collection and she knew it was in this area of debris. I asked her, how old her son was. She replied he was 15. I said back to her that my daughter aged 5 has been collecting his Lego collection for days. She was very happy to hear that. She told me, "let the Legos live on." She was happy for them to be passed on. She came by Lazy Days later to get her lunch box. (I did meet Cameron in Jan of 2018 and met him at our little local theatre. I told him this story. He remembers hearing about it from his mom. Leona and Cameron met for the first time. He told us he has more Legos from his collection. He has all the little Lego people. Weeks later he came by and dropped all the Lego people off. My girls love these Legos. Thank you to the Waldera family for letting my girls enjoy your Legos.)

Jose came home later, by another employee who gave him a ride. The girls were in bed early. They were tired from being under the sun, doing Lego collections all evening. The next two days were a routine working at Lazy Days.

WEDNESDAY SEPTEMBER 27, 2017

Marathon is no longer under any curfews and today all our kids go back to school. There were many issues going on with choosing the date kids would go back. Many parents complained that not enough kids were back or with homes and clothes to even go to school in. Other parents argued that school should have resumed earlier so kids can be back in a some-what normality of their lives, the way it was before Irma. Also to some, school was the only place at the moment where their kids could even get a hot meal and be in shelter for 6 hours a day. As usual I went with the girls to breakfast. All meals were covered till Oct. 30th for every student throughout the Keys from Elementary to High School. I was very surprised to see so many kids come back. As the girls and I say hi to many families we find out their stories and their living situations. Many of our friends are homeless. Some live with family, friends, in tents, in campers, storage areas, and even inside of businesses. Wherever they could find a spot that's where they are. At school in the cafeteria, on the stage, were donations. These items were for kids that lost it all. It was very much appreciated. Clothes, shoes, book bags (some even filled with supplies), school supplies, and more needs were all there.

While away in Alabama, Leona was worried for a little boy in her class named Liam. She had mentioned he lived on Big Pine in a home that wasn't on stilts. She was worried for him losing all he had. This first day back she spotted him and ran over to Liam. His mom was there. Leona was right. He had lost his home. It was flooded out and all their items were destroyed. Liam had no more clothes other than what he evacuated with and all else was lost. He was able to get a new book bag that day because his was gone. He was able to get new clothes and other items he needed as well. We are all thankful for the donations that came through. It was definitely needed.

Today at Marathon Community Park FEMA set up to start having people claim their losses so they could receive money back. FEMA was here for several weeks. Some didn't get the results they were looking for, while others were pleased with theirs.

Things in the community are trying to get back to normal. This will take months to recover from. Marathon doesn't look the same for us but we plan to make it look better for our family, friends, snow birds, tourists, and for us.

VALLEJO FAMILY

Angela is still in adrenaline mode. It hadn't sunk in that this had really happened. Isaak was ready and happy to go back to school today. A couple of weeks later, it had hit Isaak what had actually happened. He cried when he had seen that the camper wasn't a temporary thing for a few days, but it's going to be long term till their home gets rebuilt.

Isaak had received Legos from Lego Lands donation. Angela had filled out a form, earlier, listing what all they had lost. She had noted, he had no toys to come home too. Isaak's teacher was so kind and caring and signed him up to receive toys.

Isaak also received a toy from Telemndo TV station that came to the school. They didn't need any of the other donations brought to the school, like school supplies, book bags, and clothing, to name a few. They brought all of that with them when they left town. Isaak was just in need of things to be a kid and have fun.

SOMBRERO BEACH

BEFORE AND AFTER IRMA

BEFORE AND AFTER PICTURES

APPLIANCES OFF OF US 1 IN ISLAMORADA

OCTOBER IN THE KEYS

THE MARATHON
LIBRARY OPENED
TOWARDS THE
END OF THE MONTH

BELOW: GRASSY KEY PILE UP

MY MOMS PILE OF DEBRIS
IN HER FRONT YARD

CITY MAYOR, MICHELLE COLDIRON,
HELPED TO CARRY FURNITURE INTO
SOMBRERO BEACH COUNTRY CLUB
FOR LOCALS TO COME GET,
IF THEY WERE IN NEED.

OCTOBER IN THE KEYS

MY STORY RECAP

October 3 – A week after school started, Ariel's Karate class started back up. She was so excited. She had missed everyone. Her original leader was no longer there as he and his family had to leave the keys. Gina and her son Billy, had just passed a training course in being teachers (aka leaders) for the Dojo Karate classes, before IRMA. They knew the school would be closed for good if they didn't jump in and take over. They both decided they had to do this for themselves and the community. Karate helps many people get through different situations in different ways. Billy (young middle school boy) had told his mom they had to do this. They both went for it and re-opened the school for our community. They did change the school name to Keys Martial Arts. Thanks to Gina and Billy for taking on the school for us all.

October 5- Telemundo TV station came to Stanley Switlik Elementary. Some of the classes in the older grades were helping to roll in the boxes of toys on dolly's. The students all helped in opening doors, and unloading gifts for each other. Each child received a toy of their choice. Leona received a walking and talking dog on a leash. Ariel received an art set. All the students were so happy. For some of the kids this was the only toy they had. Many tears of happiness flooded in our kids eyes, teachers, staff members, and parents as well.

October 18- Today parents were able to come to the school cafeteria to get a costume for each child they had in the school. Over 700 costumes were donated. Some new and others gently used. Ariel was able to be Rapunzel and Leona was Aurora. These were all donated from people in Miami, the Homestead area, and a few other places I may have left out.

IRMA recovery update – Lots of businesses still closed. Our Winn-Dixie is closed. For now, we are all packed into Publix for grocery shopping. The next closest Winn-Dixie is a 20-minute drive away in Big Pine. Sombrero beach hopes to be re-opened by July 4th. All, but a few, state parks are still closed. The roads are all lined up with debris, and appliances all over just waiting to be hauled out. Sombrero Beach Country Club has the back area of their golf course loaded up with appliances. It's the dump site for those items until they're removed. The smells aren't as noticeable anymore. Loads of trucks have been coming and going constantly. Trees are growing their green back, but this time it is all over the branches, and the tree trunks are growing green. Shade from these trees are slowly coming for us. Many hotels are loaded with locals, with FEMA help, to stay there till they find housing. FEMA is helping them until Nov 1st. Kids school free lunches are now extended until November 20th. Soccer AYSO (American Youth Soccer Organization) for kids have been canceled for the year and will not start until fall of 2018. Many kids, including my own and Isaak, were very sad to skip a year of soccer. Marathon is waiting for tourists to come back as it is very empty here and everywhere else in the Keys. Many of us, like myself that work in restaurants, need tourists to help us keep going. All of our basic places for needs are open. The town is getting events back for the kids and the community to feel more at home again.

Our 1st event we had in Marathon was for Halloween. "Movie in The Park." Hotel Transylvania was played. There were snow cones, popcorn, cotton candy, glow sticks, and Publix that donated cakes and treats. It was a great celebration for our town. All of us families were brought together again and reunited. We all shared our stories together while our kids found each other to run and play with until the movie started, even then some of the kids stayed playing in the back field. Many of us were happy to see each other again and glad we were all okay. Many hugs and lots of love was exchanged tonight.

October 21st- Today was the start of burning debris from piles of garbage in open land spots. It smelled like a campfire and it wasn't the safest to be inhaling. There was a city council meeting on this, days later, and the burning came to a stop. Many locals were getting sick and complaining on safety hazards for the people in the Keys.

October 22nd – There was an ice cream social at Marathon Community Park for all the families, locals, and anyone else in town. Today was also the elementary schools Halloween carnival. All parents, staff members, and volunteers, helped to make this annual event happen for us all. IRMA wasn't going to ruin our spirits. We all came together and made two great evets happen for everyone.

October 23rd- Our lovely local library re-opens. Debris haul outs started today for all the big appliances, furniture and etc. 50 (100cubic yard) semi-trucks were working around the clock taking all our debris out of the Keys. Cable came back to the Keys as well.

Lazy Days- This week our job here has become much easier to get around the back area to better serve customers. We still have no computers and we are still hand writing it all. We now accept credit cards; this is very helpful. We did get our computer system back up and running right before Thanksgiving.

This month there was a social media post stating that some locals may come together to help have Christmas presents donated to our kids. This would be a wonderful thing to our community since many people are still not financially stable.

October 31st- Our community came together by donating tons of candy bags for our annual trick or treating fun behind the airport. This was a great event for us all. Another fun time to see families out and feeling better that things are getting better.

VALLEJO FAMILY

They are still living in the camper. "I've been having a hard time knowing we can't be in our home yet. I know we are nowhere near ready to move back inside. My son keeps asking when can we move back home? When can I have my room back? I told him we are together and that's all that matters. It was a rough month. We started to have people come, this month, to our home and fix the roof."

"Halloween made it better. Our town always has a huge trick or treating behind the airport. So glad that all the candy was donated for all the homes to hand out to the kids. We had some of our decorations from last year and we were able to decorate the camper. We had a great night. There was a huge turnout. So nice to see everyone out enjoying trick or treating."

BEN AND KRISTEN

Kristen states, "It's where I used to love to go to work, and now I almost feel.........ok, In the beginning, the stories from people, they were ok. Now it's all about FEMA. People speak of what they lost and their family and friends lost. Your heart breaks for them all. Then later you become numb to all the stories. I had this guilt in me because I didn't lose anything. I was saved. We lost a fridge because it was outside. That's all. There are still so many stories constantly coming in about people's lives. Many people ask questions and I don't always have the answers or the ones they want to hear".

They just want to be normal again. Her job that she loved so much, meeting vacationers that were excited to be on a trip, became now a burden. She now has all these depressed people. Even four months later after the storm in December into January it's been depressing. She hears stories of locals and those that are living there. Not too many tourists are in their rooms. For Christmas they got more tourists back. There are still many FEMA people in rooms waiting for their homes to be safe to live in again. FEMA had been extended to February for locals.

Kristen says, "Everyone wants their life back. we all want to feel normal".

THE VALLEJOS

THE VALLEJOS HAVE BEEN THROUGH ALOT. THEIR HOME IS SLOWLY GETTING BACK TOGETHER. THEY WERE ABLE TO PARTICIPATE IN THE ANNUAL TRICK OR TREATING EVENT BEHIND THE AIRPORT IN MARATHON. THEY KEPT THEIR SPIRITS HIGH AS WE ALL DID. THEY EVEN DECORATED THEIR CAMPER. THEY STILL HAVE A LONG WAY TO GO BUT WE ARE ALL GETTING THERE WITH COMMUNITY HELP.
PICTURED ABOVE IS ANEGLAS SON ISAAK AND HIS FRIEND

NOVEMBER IN
THE KEYS

NOVEMBER IN THE KEYS

MY STORY

November 1st – Things are starting to feel better around town. People seem to all be back to their homes and getting them fixed up, while others are getting them demolished. People are all still working together as teams to help each other out. It's nice to see such a community impact lives.

There's still no Bealls, IHOP, Dollar Tree, Burger King, Wendy's, Winn-Dixie, Advance Auto Parts, Nicks Gym, and more…. Still no fun on Sombrero Beach yet. Many places are still closed. Jose and I drive once a week to Key Largo to go to some of the places that aren't open here but they are up there. It was crazy, we had to drive the extra distance to save money and get items we couldn't get in Marathon.

Veterans Day weekend Marathon had "Taste of the Islands". This is an annual event where restaurants come together to promote their best dishes. Awards are given at the end. This is a one-day event and it was a success. In spite of the hurricane it was a great turnout. This event was put together last minute in about a week of time.

VALLEJO FAMILY

This month was Rough as well. A little sigh of relief that their patio was built up and the roof was completed. They Still felt they were a step closer to moving in side for thanksgiving but it didn't happen. The 3 of them shared the holiday with family in Miami. This family still continues to be in their camper and doing their daily life routines. They were just waiting for dry wall to be done, which happened after Thanksgiving.

"Places around town have started to open more now. Jobs are gradually coming back for our friends, neighbors, and our community. This month was nice to be able to get to places that we all needed."

DECEMBER IN
THE KEYS

DECEMBER IN THE KEYS

MY STORY

This month we finally get some progress for us here in the keys. Our Bealls opened up this month. Dollar Tree opened in January. Sombrero Beach re-opened just a little before Christmas. Still no news om IHOP. Burger King will not be re-opening at all. Wendy's had an article out in the weekly paper that it will become a Pollo Tropical in the later months. Winn-Dixie (we found out in February) it will re-open in fall of 2018. There are still so many more damaged homes and businesses that weren't mentioned in this book. Many of those will be torn down, if they haven't been already. Other places will just sit there destroyed. Homes will sit abandoned. Many places in the Keys won't be cleaned as it was before. Just walking around you will still find Irma remains. You can walk around months later close to summer and you will still find dried sea grass, and items that didn't get picked up from the loads hauled out. It will most likely take a couple of years for it all to be back as it was. Surely with time, we will get there.

Hotels for locals were extended till February and then it was time to make room for the tourist's season. All school lunches were covered till Jan. 31st. It was nice to see kids school lunches go for a few months being free.

Things really started to pop back to normal this month for the community. We had several Christmas events in the town of Marathon. It was great to see all our yearly ones come back to resume again this year. Thanks to Marathon for keeping each other so strong. We are KEYS STRONG.

VALLEJO FAMILY

"It was nice to see dry wall all done and ceilings painted. We moved our kitchen things back into the kitchen. We can cook in our home now. Still can't sleep over night there yet. We do have a Christmas tree up. So glad to see that there were Santa events around town for all of us to get together at. Courtney and I had taken our kids to the local bank to see Santa, get pictures done, and have cookies. We went for ice cream later after that. It was a good time. Things are slowly getting better for us. We hope to be home in another week and have it all done. My son still made perfect attendance, received a reader's award, and AB honor roll. With all we have been through we are a strong family and we are doing okay now. Lastly, we did get to finally move into our home for good, the week of Christmas. It was such a gift for us as a family to receive. We got our rooms back and started to get things to how they were before. "

BIG PINE
THIS ROOF IS GONE

MARATHON CANAL PHOTOS BELOW

THIS MESS WAS HERE FOR MONTHS ALONG US 1 NEAR 7 MILE BRIDGE HEADED SOUTH

THIS PICTURE WAS TAKEN AT COCO PLUM BEACH. ALL THE GREEN HAS BEEN STRIPPED AWAY. ITS ALL BARE LIKE A WINTER SCENE IN SUMMER HEAT

ALL OF THIS DEBRIS WAS SEEN ALONG US 1 AFTER PASSING BIG PINE KEY

FKEC ANNUAL HOLIDAY LIGHTING

FLORIDA KEYS ELECTRIC
(FKEC)
DONATED FOOD AND DRINKS
TO THE COMMUNITY FOR THE
ANNUAL LIGHTING OF THE
CHRISTMAS LIGHTS
AT FKEC.

MICHELLE COLDIRON
, CITY MAYOR
OF MARATHON,WAS HERE
TO SHARE THE OPENING
OF THE LIGHTS
AT FKEC.

MR AND MRS. CLAUS WERE
THERE TO SEE ALL THE
CHILDREN.THIS WAS A
MAGICAL MOMENT
FOR OUR KIDS

OF COURSE WE HAD
SNOW FOAM
PROVIDED FOR
THE CHILDREN.

FROM COMMUNITY TO COMMUNITY

STUFFED BAGS FROM MASS.

$1,000 to Ashley Keeney , president of the Stanley Switlik PTO. This donation was raised by the students and staff of Hugh J Boyd elementary school in Seaside Heights, New Jersey. Thank you Miriam Schneider for heading up the hurricane relief fund raiser

QUILTS DONATED FROM OHIO CHURCH TO SWITLIK ELEMENTARY SCHOOL

DONATIONS TO THE KEYS

- (picture of community to community title page)- Book bags came from other schools in Seekonk MA, to our elementary school in Marathon Florida. The book bags were decorated by students and then stuffed with school supplies. Stanley Switlik kids grades K-2 received these book bags.
- Toys pictured above - These toys are only a few of the hundreds Switlik School received from Telemundo TV station. The camera crew came in and recorded our student's reactions as they were handed gifts. It was a great day for all our staff and kids at the school.
- Books pictured above – Hundreds of books were sent in from other Florida schools for our students and school library to keep. Some books were new and others were gently used. Our school was very happy to get books. These were needed.
- Keys Martial Arts picture above- Will Mc Caskey Is a past student of the Keys Martial Arts school. He lives in Missouri where he heard of the hurricane hitting the keys. He started a go fund me account for the school here. He raised enough money to buy all the students at the school new equipment and weapons to work with. He stayed with the school until the end of January to help all the leaders and students learn how to use the new weapons.
- Girl Scout Troops - Girl scouts in California sent Marathons Girl Scouts Troop letters in hopes that all the girls are doing better and they're sorry for their loss. Money was donated to our Marathon Troop to buy new sashes and vests as many were lost in the storm.
- MM50 project in Marathon - This lovely group of people collected donations from all over the state of Florida. Donations came from other schools that collected Christmas gifts for Stanley Switlik School. Presents were handed out the last week of school before Christmas break.
- School raised money – Students and staff from a North Carolina Elementary school, raised $2,054 for Stanley Switlik School. Thanks to this school for their thoughtfulness.
- Americare for Women - Woman Kind in Key West received donations from Americare. $10,000 in Nexplanon (3-year birth control) and IUD's (5 and 10-year birth controls), and $15,000 in donated medications. It has saved countless women thousands of dollars. All these women are so grateful for the money saved. Many thanks to Americare for helping Women Kind.
- Food for Florida- Thank-you food for Florida. Thousands of families were paid back through food stamps due to Irma taking away food from their homes and losing food that was in cold storage spots. This greatly helped so many in need for food funding.

THANKS AGAIN TO ALL WHO DONATED TO THE KEYS IN ANY KIND OF WAY. WE CAN'T THANK YOU ENOUGH!!

A FEW HURRICANE IRMA FACTS

Irma began August 30th ,2017 near the Cape Verde Islands. The 4th hurricane of the season, 9th named storm. Irma developed from a tropical wave that developed off the west African coast two days earlier. It rapidly strengthened into a category 2 storm within 24 hours. (Source: World vision>Disaster-relief-new-stories)

* Hurricane Irma is the strongest Atlantic basin hurricane ever recorded outside the Gulf of Mexico and the Caribbean Sea. It lasted from August 31st – until September 11th. It stretched 650 miles east to west. It affected 9 US states. (Source: CNN.Com>specials>hurricane-IRMA)

* Tropical storm force winds extended 185 miles from the center. Storm surges were 20ft above normal tide levels. (Source: "Hot water ahead for hurricane Irma," NASA, Sept.7,2017) Irma held 7 trillion watts of energy. Sept 6,2017

* 6.5 million Floridians had been ordered to evacuate by Governor, Rick Scott.

* Over 70,000 people were in 385 shelters

* Near 114,000 people were in 500 shelters statewide in Florida by Sunday Morning Sept 10th, 2017

* Herd of 949 Endangered Key Deer survived Irma's storm.

* Since Nov., the number of boats damaged or destroyed in category 4 Irma and pulled from the ocean, has gone up by 315. As of Dec. 1,671 boats had been taken out of the keys waters by State and federal agencies. (Source; "Fl. Keysnews.com")

* 672 vessels have been taken from the waters in Marathon and Big Pine Key. If boats weren't claimed by owners, they were crushed in a staging area with an excavator. There were 7 staging areas throughout the county. (Source:"Fl.keysnews.com")

* 134 people lost their life in this Hurricane. 72 were killed in Florida. 10 of the 72 were elderly victims who died in a nursing home north of Miami. 8 of the 72 died in the Florida Keys. The remaining deaths occurred in the Caribbean. The causes of death in Florida: drowning, trauma injuries, heart attack, and carbon monoxide poisoning – some used their generators for indoor electricity. (Source: phys.org)

DESTRUCTION OF THE KEYS CHART NUMBERS

CITY	UNAFFECTED	AFFECTED	MINOR	MAJOR	DESTROYED
KEY LARGO	2581	3992	326	75	46
MARATHON	0	4018	829	1402	394
BIG PINE KEY	264	1538	663	299	473
KEY WEST	0	11625	282	39	23

GRAND TOTAL FOR ALL THE KEYS:

	UNAFFECTED	AFFECTED	MINOR	MAJOR	DESTROYED
	5467	27649	5391	2977	1179

Picture below credited to BOCC

Restaurants in the Keys

Ocean Beach Glunz and Havana Jacks

Looe Key Tiki across from Boondocks

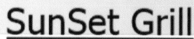

SunSet Grill

Ocean Front Park dock buckles up

FARNMOST

Publix delivers food

Welcome to FLORIDA

THE SUNSHINE

CLOSED FOR REMODE

LAZY DAYS new

Ocean Front Dining

The abover ground pool is under water here

Before

Sombrero Beach

Before

After

After

PIC·COLLAGE

FEMA Lunch

"FEMA LUNCH"
CHEESY TUNA
MELT

nails in tires

WE ARE MARATHON STRONG!

BAHIA HONDA STATE PARK

crackers

MREs

CRACKERS

Sweet and Sour Chicken Meal

fig bar

ORIGINAL Skittles

Islamorada

BOIL WATER ADVISORY

CURFEW 10PM TO DAWN

H

CLOSED CAPE CITY HALL 24/7

Several feets of sand

yucky

NOW OPEN! we are Selling GAS!

Shed moved across the street

this house moved off its foundation. It landed across the street

The Marathon Airport housed Volunteers in tents

someone's house

BURGER KING

Burger King wont be re-opening

CREDITS

SPECIAL THANKS TO ALL THOSE WHO PROVIDED PICTURES FOR THIS BOOK:

MICHELLE COLDIRON, ANGELA VALLEJO, RONNIE ASHLEY, NAYDA BUTTNER, LORETTA ALKALAY, MARCEL DELORM, BOCC, BERNIE ORNELAS, DERRICK JOHNSON, AYDEN CHILD, KATHIA MOSCOSO, GEO TOTH, GANINE DERLETH, SHELLY STEINBRUGGE, MARK SMITH AND TO ALL ELSE I MAY HAVE MISSED.

SPECIAL THANKS TO THOSE FOR EDITING MY BOOK

ABIGAIL JOHNS EDWARDS, MIMI QUINONES, SHERRY HOLMES,

ANGELA VALLEJO

SPECIAL THANKS TO TWO AMAZING GUYS WHO HELPED WITH TECHNICAL PROGRAMMING

THE WHOLE WAY IN THE BOOK PROCESS

WARREN AND PATRICK MOSES

SPECIAL THANKS TO BUSINESSES THAT HAD THEIR STORIES IN THE BOOK

LAZY DAYS SOUTH, SEA DELL MOTEL, STANLEY SWILIK, FKEC, KEYS MARTIAL ARTS, AND MORE

THANKS TO THE FAMILIES WHO SHARED THEIR STORY

THE VALLEJO FAMILY, BEN (BONGO) AND KRISTEN TURNER, AND THE FAMILIES

WHO HAD SMALLER STORIES TO SHARE.

SPECIAL THANKS TO ALL OF MY FRIENDS AND FAMILY WHO WERE IN THE BOOK AND SUPPORTED ME THROUGH IT ALL

THANK YOU AGAIN TO ALL OF THOSE WHO HAD A PART IN MY BOOK.

THANKS TO THOSE WHO ENCOURAGED ME TO KEEP WRITING.

THANKS TO THOSE WHO ALLOWED THEIR NAMES AND FACES TO BE A PART OF THIS STORY.

THANKS TO ANYONE ELSE THAT I MAY HAVE LEFT OUT.

THIS BOOK WOULDN'T HAVE BEEN POSSIBLE WITHOUT ALL YOUR HELP.

BAHIA HONDA STATE PARK

crackers

MREs

Sweet and Sour Chicken Meal

fig bar

Skittles

Islamorada

Several feets of sand

yucky raisins

BOIL WATER ADVISORY

CURFEW 10PM TO DAWN

H

CLOSED
CAPE CITY HALL 24/7

NOW OPEN! we are Selling GAS!

Shed moved across the street

this house moved off its foundation. It landed across the street

The Marathon Airport housed Volunteers in tents

someone's house

BURGER KIM

Burger King wont be re-opening

CREDITS

SPECIAL THANKS TO ALL THOSE WHO PROVIDED PICTURES FOR THIS BOOK:

MICHELLE COLDIRON, ANGELA VALLEJO, RONNIE ASHLEY, NAYDA BUTTNER, LORETTA ALKALAY, MARCEL DELORM, BOCC, BERNIE ORNELAS, DERRICK JOHNSON, AYDEN CHILD, KATHIA MOSCOSO, GEO TOTH, GANINE DERLETH, SHELLY STEINBRUGGE, MARK SMITH AND TO ALL ELSE I MAY HAVE MISSED.

SPECIAL THANKS TO THOSE FOR EDITING MY BOOK

ABIGAIL JOHNS EDWARDS, MIMI QUINONES, SHERRY HOLMES,

ANGELA VALLEJO

SPECIAL THANKS TO TWO AMAZING GUYS WHO HELPED WITH TECHNICAL PROGRAMMING

THE WHOLE WAY IN THE BOOK PROCESS

WARREN AND PATRICK MOSES

SPECIAL THANKS TO BUSINESSES THAT HAD THEIR STORIES IN THE BOOK

LAZY DAYS SOUTH, SEA DELL MOTEL, STANLEY SWILIK, FKEC, KEYS MARTIAL ARTS, AND MORE

THANKS TO THE FAMILIES WHO SHARED THEIR STORY

THE VALLEJO FAMILY, BEN (BONGO) AND KRISTEN TURNER, AND THE FAMILIES

WHO HAD SMALLER STORIES TO SHARE.

SPECIAL THANKS TO ALL OF MY FRIENDS AND FAMILY WHO WERE IN THE BOOK AND SUPPORTED ME THROUGH IT ALL

THANK YOU AGAIN TO ALL OF THOSE WHO HAD A PART IN MY BOOK.

THANKS TO THOSE WHO ENCOURAGED ME TO KEEP WRITING.

THANKS TO THOSE WHO ALLOWED THEIR NAMES AND FACES TO BE A PART OF THIS STORY.

THANKS TO ANYONE ELSE THAT I MAY HAVE LEFT OUT.

THIS BOOK WOULDN'T HAVE BEEN POSSIBLE WITHOUT ALL YOUR HELP.

Made in the USA
Columbia, SC
22 July 2018